A HOME FRONT
DIARY
1914–1918

D1136668

A HOME FRONT DIARY
1914–1918

LILLIE SCALES

AMBERLEY

First published 2014

Amberley Publishing
The Hill, Stroud
Gloucestershire, GL5 4EP

www.amberley-books.com

Copyright © Peter Scales, Kate Scales and the estate of Lillie Scales 2014

The right of Peter Scales, Kate Scales and the estate of Lillie Scales to be
identified as the Authors of this work has been asserted in accordance with
the Copyrights, Designs and Patents Act 1988.

All rights reserved. No part of this book may be reprinted
or reproduced or utilised in any form or by any electronic,
mechanical or other means, now known or hereafter invented,
including photocopying and recording, or in any information
storage or retrieval system, without the permission in writing
from the Publishers.

British Library Cataloguing in Publication Data.
A catalogue record for this book is available from the British Library.

ISBN 978 1 4456 1896 8 (paperback)
ISBN 978 1 4456 1908 8 (ebook)

Typeset in 10pt on 12pt Sabon.
Typesetting and Origination by Amberley Publishing.
Printed in the UK.

Contents

Introduction

Maria Elizabeth Scales, known to all as Lillie, was an upper-middle-class lady living in London during the First World War. Born in 1868, she was already aged forty-six when the war began. Upon marrying George McArthur Scales in 1890, she moved with him to Elm Bank, Hornsey Lane in London; as a result, she was at the very centre of wartime activity. Although neither of them could take a front-line role, George and Lillie were determined to play an active part in the war effort: Lillie started a first aid course, and the couple felt it was their duty as patriotic citizens to provide a temporary home for refugees and soldiers.

Recognising that the First World War would play an incredibly important part in the history of the nation, she started to write these memoirs on its second anniversary, in August 1916, basing the early years on her own and George's diaries. She ends them in 1919 after the signing of the Peace Treaty and the repatriation of the surviving Anzac boys, and the reader is thus offered a complete picture of the war, from the initial fears up until the return of some semblance of normality.

Within the pages of her diary, Lillie wrote about everything that came to mind, and the result is an intimate and honest portrayal of the day-to-day life of an upper-middle-class family during the First World War. Horrific stories of attempted Zeppelin raids on Christmas Day 1914 (and the real thing in August and September the following year: 'We saw a hole made by a bomb large enough for a cart to go in it') are intermingled with the immediate concerns about rationing and money, showing that life had to, and did, go on despite the significant social upheaval. The cost of coal might have doubled, but it was only 'unpatriotic people who are not attempting to ration themselves' and 'all honourable people who realise the condition of things are doing their best to keep to them'.

It was George and Lillie's family and business connections in Australia that persuaded them to welcome the Anzacs and other Colonial soldiers into their home when they were on leave. The couple had no children of their own, but the boys they took in seem to have regarded Lillie as a mother figure. A letter from one of them in 1949, included at the end of this book, illustrates the long-lasting relationships that Lillie formed during the war years. Her warmth encouraged them to be open about their experiences of war; as a result, Lillie's memoirs provide a compelling insight into life on the

Front Line ('Of 42 officers in his battalion only two remained, of whom he is one.').

Lillie and her immediate family were not untouched by the war. Zeppelin raids were more common than one might assume, and influenza was rife. The stress of war on the home population led to her own family tragedy, and the difficulties in dealing with life and death under such circumstances are described thoughtfully and emotionally. Her mother and father both died during the war, as did many of the brothers of men who stayed with her and George, though in vastly different circumstances.

Of great historical importance is the insight these memoirs give into the impact the war had on social attitudes. The division within society is made clear through events related in the diary, from the loss of maids to the triple alliance strikes for better working conditions. The memoirs are very much of their time, and highlight the hopes and fears of a bygone era. Technological advances, such as the aeroplane ('I wonder if I shall ever go in one'), spelt the beginning of a new – and, for some people, frightening – age, one in which class divides were transcended ('She showed Reg that she was "fond of him" (!) and he went head over heels … but no girl of his class would have acted as she did.'), and government attitudes changed dramatically. The old order was changing, and the First World War was the catalyst.

I came across these memoirs among other family 'memorabilia' passed down to me from my great uncle George McArthur Scales. They provide such a unique insight into life in Britain 100 years ago, and detail so many aspects of the war from such a variety of perspectives, that I wanted to share them. They are a fascinating and valuable read for anyone interested in the First World War and its implications for the generations to come.

My grateful thanks go to my daughter Kate for her diligence in deciphering and typing up Lillie's diaries. Thanks, too, to Nicola and Emily of Amberley for their patience with me and their expertise.

Peter Scales

Dramatis Personae

Lillie (Scales) married George McArthur Scales in 1890 and wrote these diaries during the First World War.

George (McArthur Scales) became a partner in the family firm, before marrying Lillie in 1890.

Charles James Thomas: Lillie's father, married to Mary Matilda.

Ethel and Bernard Matthews: Lillie's sister and her husband.

Mr G. J. Scales: George Johnston, George's father and founder of the family firm, McDonald Scales & Co.

Harold and Florence Scales: Lillie's brother-in-law and his wife.

Harold and Maud Thomas: Lillie's brother and his wife.

Mary and Courtney Scales: Lillie's sister-in-law and nephew. Mary married William, George's brother.

Millicent Berry: an Australian relation who could not get back to Australia during the war and so stayed with Lillie and George.

Bert Chesters: an Australian soldier who stayed with Lillie and George in 1918.

Cecil Dunn: an Australian soldier who stayed with Lillie and George in 1916. The Dunns' father was an old friend of George's.

Gainor Jackson: a New Zealand soldier who visited Lillie and George in 1918.

Guy Wagg: a New Zealand soldier who stayed with Lillie and George in 1916.

Harry Brooker: an Australian soldier who stayed with Lillie in 1918, and brought his wife Betty to meet them before returning to Australia.

Jack Dunn: an Australian soldier who stayed with Lillie and George in 1917. The Dunns' father was an old friend of George's.

Jim Gibb: an Australian soldier who performed as part of the 'Anzac Coves' and stayed with Lillie and George in 1918.

Murray Sinclair: an Australian soldier, and friend of Bert Chester, who visited Lillie and George in 1918.

Reginald Dunn: an Australian soldier who stayed with Lillie and George in 1916. The Dunns' father was an old friend of George's.

Rod Piper: an Australian soldier, and friend of Cecil Dunn, who visited Lillie and George in 1917.

Will Wagg: a New Zealand soldier who visited Lillie and George in 1918.

Lillie's Journal

Journal commenced August 15th, 1916. The following are extracts from my diary.

July 28th, Tuesday, 1914. George poorly in bed. Very quiet day. It seems extraordinary that we had no idea of what was coming upon us. I am writing this on Sunday, Aug 2nd.

29th, Wednesday. George much better and came downstairs. Ethel rang up on the telephone to say that she was worried about Harold, and that was actually the first I had heard of the possibility of war. They were having a dreadful day on the Stock Exchange. No one had thought there could be a European war, but on Wednesday our eyes were opened. 7 firms on the Stock Exchange were hammered, including the great Stonehams. Rang Harold up in the evening. He had got on better than he had feared. Harold Scales came in for a long talk.

Thursday, July 30th. George went to town. War news very alarming, but great hopes of settlement.

Friday, July 31st. War news very menacing. George telephoned to me in the morning to say that the Kaiser's brother had gone to Russia on an errand of peace, and that the Stock Exchange had closed. An unknown thing in the memory of man. It seems that 25 of the leading firms say that if they did not close the Exchange they would all be hammered, and with them three-quarters of the Stock Exchange. This crisis has come with incredible swiftness.

I saw Mrs Carr in the morning. Mary, Courtney and Hamilton Gailey came to lunch and Mary G. and Louie afterwards. Last night Mr and Mrs Gregory came to dinner.

Saturday, August 1st. George and I took the bus from Crouch End to Blackheath. It took 2 hours. We saw a placard at the Mansion House – 'King intervenes' – and felt more hopeful. Mother told us of dear Harold's great trouble and how they had helped him. They are a splendid Father and Mother. Harold is very brave. Maud naturally very depressed but very sweet and nice to Harold. H. and M., Father and George went for a motor ride. We came home at 7. No definite news in papers but grave fears.

Sunday, August 2nd. Harold Scales came in with Sunday paper. <u>Germany has declared war on Russia</u>. Service was held in the schoolroom, as the church is being cleaned. Mr Lyne turned the service into a prayer meeting. Mrs Cowlishaw and Mrs Morell crying 1 on each side of me. Mr Lyne spoke of the imminence of the danger, that the Cabinet was then sitting to decide if England must fight, an unprecedented hour for a council – and that our fleet is mobilising. He came from Jersey last night, and search lights were playing all over the Channel. If England goes to war it will not be lightheartedly. How we prayed that we might be delivered from war. Mrs Norman Sargant told me coming home that they had lost every penny. The whole position is inconceivable. So sudden!

Monday, August 3rd. We heard that Germany had declared war on France, and had invaded France, Luxembourg and Belgium, and we felt it must mean war for us and yet we felt that it would have been more natural to be fighting on Germany's side than against her. We little knew what her soul was like.

Tuesday, August 4th. I went down to the grocer's and ordered in about £30 of provisions. A day or two afterwards the papers protested about this being done and said it was unpatriotic. However, I had done it then. They had spent the day at the office discussing how to insure against war risks. The rate in the morning was

3%, then 5%, then 10%. People coming home from the Continent had dreadful experiences. They told of stacks of luggage on the French wharfs unclaimed – including motor cars. Dr and Mrs Bonsfield got out of Germany by the last train. They had fights to get into their trains, and could get nothing to eat. The Worringhams were weeks in Switzerland before they could get away. Used up all their money, then were days getting home when at last a train started, and had to sit up all the way. No one could hear from, or get messages to, their friends.

On the stroke of 12 p.m. having waited till the last moment for Germany's reply to her note, Great Britain declared war on Germany. There was no alternative in honour.

August 5th. We were to have gone to Wanstead to stay for a few days, but felt everything was so uncertain and unsettled that returned home in the evening. The morning placards had 'Fierce naval battle raging in North Sea'. It was not true, but everyone feels they do not know what may happen next. I asked the maids if they would like to go to their homes. But they were very sensible.

August 7th. I went up to the Polytechnic for 'First Aid' classes. In my class there were 200 ladies. Everything was in the greatest confusion. Over 1,000 ladies had come, and they had not expected more than 50. We had 5 lectures on consecutive days on first aid – and then there was an exam. I did not take it, as it was absurd to rush it like that, and if I had managed to pass, I should not have remembered anything. The next week, 5 lectures on home nursing and an exam. Absurd, and the classes were too large to practise bandaging etc.

August 8th. George and I went to Woolwich. It was a wonderful sight to see the guns and the soldiers. The horses, many of them, looked as if they had just been commandeered – very rough. The Rayners had had 1 of their horses taken. We did not realise what a tiny army we were opposing to Germany's millions. But it was an army of heroes, every man of it. Some of the troops were going to Belgium, some to France – Newcastle – Harwich etc. King's Cross station was closed to the public, and during the following weeks stations were frequently closed and it was difficult to get about because of the movements of the troops. One day going from Blackheath to London, George was turned out with all the other men at New Cross.

On August 15th we heard of the fall of Liege after its gallant defence and on August 16th our expeditionary force landed in France. It had been mobilised and despatched most splendidly and rapidly and when the French saw the commissariat they said it looked like a trade invasion. Motor vans and lorries had been commandeered from the trading houses all over the country and the vans of drapers, brewers, millers, removers etc., emblazoned with their names, enlivened the procession. But it is a comfort to know that the commissariat, and the medical and sanitary arrangements, have all been as good as it has been possible to make them all through the war – even though the poor men have got sick of plum jam.

During the next few days the Germans overran Belgium. On the 20th they occupied Brussels – the 22nd, on the placards was seen 'Germans at Ostend', that brilliant pleasure resort where we had stayed with Mr G. J. Scales. We went to dinner at Mrs Sargant's that night and were all very depressed.

Father and Mother were to have gone to Sidmouth for their holiday but cancelled their arrangements, and Harold and Florence went to Brighton instead of Aldeburgh as the latter is on the east coast. Most people cancelled their holidays, many for business reasons, others because travelling was so difficult.

Intercession services were being held in many places, and we had one on the 21st, for one feels that one's only hope is in God and that He <u>will</u> defend the right. A beautiful intercession form of service had been published by the SPCK.

Directly war was declared there was a most wonderful rush of men to enlist. Almost every young fellow we knew volunteered the first week of war. Both George's and my brothers are too old, of course. My Harold has been accepted for 'sedentary service abroad', but he is now [1916] over 40 and such a delicate man that I cannot help hoping he will not be called upon. But all our young cousins volunteered. Howard, Fred and Geoffrey Savage. Ronald, Godfrey, Bernard, Gerard and Bertram Thomas [aged 41]. Bernard Douthwaite, Hamilton Gailey, Allister and Geoffrey Keble White. Geoffrey Cather, Courtney Scales, Graham and Tom Shillington [Graham is Tom's father, and Tom at one time was his father's superior officer]. Dermot Cather.

The recruiting offices were besieged and one of the saddest and yet most thrilling sights to me was to see parties of those young fellows who had just volunteered being marched from the recruiting office – perhaps 30, 50 or 100 of them – in all sorts of dress – top hats, caps, soft hats, morning coats, jackets, shabby men and 'nuts', labourers, clerks, partners in great city businesses – hooligans, all mixed up, marching side by side, all having made the great decision, ready to lay down their lives for their country, and you could see this in many of their faces. No bands to help them along, just 2 or 3 soldiers with them. And in all the city squares you saw them drilling – at first without uniforms, in their city clothes, then half the men in uniforms and half not. It made one's heart ache. For these men had never thought of being soldiers, but they came gladly when their country needed them and these citizen armies of ours have also proved to be armies of heroes upholding the very grandest traditions of the Empire. Men that make one glow with pride and thankfulness.

Of course there are many stories of recruiting offices that disgust one. Street went to volunteer. He filled up 5 sheets of questions and then the man said, 'Are you willing to be vaccinated?' Street thought it was an optional matter so said 'no', and the man told him to clear out then, which Street promptly did, being angry. While he was waiting previously a gentleman came in. He had spent 2 days going from recruiting office to recruiting office and he had been sent from one to another, wasting hours in each. He threw his papers across the office saying he would waste no more time over it if they did not want him – and left. A gentleman known to a friend of ours offered his motor and himself to the War Office. He wrote many times but received no reply. Finally he wrote and told Lord Kitchener. The following day he had a letter from the War Office telling him to call. He waited an hour or two, then was called into a room and was blackguarded up and down hill by the occupant for having written to Lord Kitchener. He still was patriotic enough to give his car. Dr de Mouilpied [of Jersey] was appointed to an important scientific post in France and had to have a commission. After much delay a letter came from the War Office to say that commissions could only be given to British subjects! Of course he got it eventually.

August 24th. The great retreat from Mons began. I shall never forget seeing the placard in Portland Place as I went to my first aid lecture – 'British Retreating' – but even then we did not at all realise the danger though we were very anxious. But now we know that that retreat was one of the most wonderful feats of any army and the devotion and heroism of our men glorious. And then the way in which, within a few miles of Paris, the Allies turned and slowly forced back the enemy was miraculous.

A gentleman said to Dr Bonsfield 'why does not God work a miracle on the side of justice' and Dr Bonsfield said, 'If you want a miracle you have it in the retreat of the Germans when there was practically nothing between them and Paris.' The Allies' line was the <u>thinnest</u>. At one point on the retreat it was so thin that they scraped up every man, even calling the cooks out.

There have been many explanations of the Germans' panic given. They saw a phantom army rushing up – cavalry leading – the old bowmen of Crecy appeared and fought for us – a company of angels was seen between us and our enemies. 'The Russians' appeared and they were afraid of their flank being turned. It is a great mystery, but I suppose that an army did unexpectedly appear on their flank and they thought great reinforcements had come up. A few weeks ago I was reading the account of the funeral of the general who was responsible for the defence of Paris, and the taxi drivers of Paris had made a special request to be represented in the procession because he had trusted them and called them out to convey an army round behind the Allies' lines in great haste and that this had saved Paris. This may be the solution of the mystery.

August 30th. On Sunday evening Harold came in with a most terrible newspaper account of the retreat and I think it was the next day it was all confirmed in *The Times*. *The Times* got into terrible trouble about it, but it had been passed by the Censor and there is no doubt it was perfectly true. But everyone was appalled and of course our troops then were still retreating. Another arose – that extraordinary legend and rumour about the arrival of 250,000 Russians, which was believed by practically everyone. One heard such circumstantial accounts of them that even now the whole thing is a mystery. We heard of them first on that Sunday night. Hamilton Gailey telephoned that he had been having dinner with a friend in town. The latter had come up from Tunbridge Wells to meet him, but had been very late for his train had been held up for troop trains, and these trains were full of strange bearded men, talking a foreign language and 'smelling like nothing on earth'. The station master said they were Russians, landed in the north of Scotland and going through to France. And on all sides this was confirmed. Miss Sutherland told me how a friend of hers had seen them going through

Newcastle. The station master at Hither Green told Honor Matthews of these trains of Russians, a lot of them had crossed the Channel in a ship commanded by a friend of Bernard's – a lot of them were in camp on Salisbury Plain. A cousin of Maud's said that the camp was next to his – and there were numberless other stories and even a picture in the *Daily Mail* of 'Russians fording a river in France'. News came from Italy that 250,000 Russians had passed through England to France.

I asked Mr Dixon of the Home Office what he thought and he said that if it were only a rumour it was the best-founded one he had ever heard. Father was the only one I met who did not believe in them, and he got quite angry about it. Everyone talked and argued about the Russians. Then all their accoutrement was said to have gone down in a great ship that was lost in the north of Scotland. People even saw the ships they had come in!

On September 6th 1914 the battle of the Marne began and on September 15th the battle of the Aisne and then the great siege battle began and the lines are about the same today [August 1916] as they were then – in the west.

I would dearly have liked to take up regular war work but my time was already more than full with church work which it seemed impossible to give up, especially as so many people left church work to do war work. But I should certainly have tried to do more than I have done if I had not had an enlarged thyroid gland which obliged me to take a good deal of rest for a year, and then when I began work it came on again after a few months and I have now been hardly doing anything for 5 months, which is fairly sickening when everyone is so busy.

On August 25th I had a working meeting to which about 35 came. We had several machines and made about 80 or 90 bed jackets, shirts etc., the ladies taking them home to finish. So many things are needed for the hospitals and these garments were for Mary Tait who is helping at a large field hospital. Then we bought a lot of wool and with Mrs Lyne's help I got out wool for socks, scarves etc. and directions to numbers for her and my women and girls, who were delighted to knit for the soldiers and sailors. I sent Miss McDonald 90 scarves and pairs of socks for the navy, Miss James 30 for her brother's regiment, Mrs Cather 30 and many more later. We also got to know from the men who had gone from our church what they would like for Christmas and sent it to them. We could send 7 lbs for a shilling, and not more than 11 lbs. George found out for me from the Navy League the right things to make. Scarves 2 yards long and wide, and socks large, of thick wool. He also, on August 31st, went to Hudson's Depository, Victoria, which had been opened as a sort of receiving house for the Belgian refugees. The poor creatures arrived there after several days of misery on boats, and waiting for boats, without any luggage, and not enough clothing, and Red Cross nurses and ladies were there feeding and looking after them. George went at once round the manufacturers and got hair brushes, combs, toothbrushes, handkerchiefs etc. and I set to work to collect clothes, principally night and children's clothes. By September 3rd I had got together about 80 garments which we packed up in cardboard boxes, and filled Harold's car. I have regretted those cardboard boxes ever since!

George for the last 2 years has taken the organ 3 times a week at St Giles's church, Cripplegate, as Mr Moody, the organist, is engaged in war work and if George did not play, there would be no music for the services. The organ is a fine one, and George loves playing it and loves the old church too and likes the vicar, Mr Morgan Brown. He will be quite sorry to give it up again. [George writes 'Not yet given up Jan 1922 nor on July 1st 1928'.]

September 13th, 1914, Sunday. Mr Gregory read at the service the names of 28 young men who had enlisted, belonging to our congregation. At the beginning of this year, 1916, 126 had volunteered, and on August 4th 1916 when we had our intercession service, the list numbered over 140. (January 1917. 170 have enlisted from Archway Road.)

October 1914. In the early part of October 1914 the Belgian refugees began to come over in such numbers that private hospitality was asked for them, and the response was wonderful. We all felt that it was owing to Belgium that our own land had been saved from the cruel Huns and that the sorrows and sufferings of Belgium would have been ours too if it had not been for the bravery of them and their King.

Houston and Ellie Hardy took a family of 11 into their house for 10 days until a place could be found for them. At Aldwych in the great skating rink and houses adjoining, the Belgian headquarters for refugees was established. The boats bringing them were met by voluntary workers at Harwich. They were given food and sent in special trains to London, and conveyed to Aldwych. There you could see them in hundreds, sitting in forlorn little family groups, looking so sad, as well they might after the horrors and privations they had been through. There they were fed and clothed by ladies, and people came to choose whom they would invite to their houses. All the Belgians had to be registered at Aldwych, and Aldwych became responsible for them, for there was a danger of spies. We heard many stories of people getting spies into their houses. One lady took 2 nuns. One day she heard some curious noise in their bedroom, and knocked at their door. There was no reply, and she opened the door and looked in and saw one of the nuns shaving. One spy was taken through a girl in a tube train seeing a man's boot under the skirt of a nun. Ellie and Houston Hardy went up to Aldwych and saw the Hamel family and took them straight to their home. It consisted of Monsieur and Madame, Madame's sister, and 8 children, from 14 downwards. Monsieur was a professor from Malines, and he and his family had escaped out of the city as the Germans entered. We went up to see them, and George to talk to them, for they did not understand English. The children were sweet. After a time Dr Bonsfield with the help of subscriptions took a furnished house for them, where they are still. Only Monsieur has returned to Malines.

The rush at Aldwych was so great that other houses were opened all over London to which the poor things were sent in batches. Educated refined people mixed up with the lowest of the low and the Belgians can be low – much worse than our poorest. A house opposite to Mr and Mrs Lyne was filled with these Belgians. Mrs Lyne could talk French and went over and found that there were no fires, beds – or food. The Aldwych Committee could not help it – the people were arriving in thousands. Private people were supplying such houses with furniture and doing all that was possible. Mrs Lyne sent across all the food she could get (it was Sunday), and took into her house three delightful people – a Mr and Madame Vanderbilt and their son from the trenches in front of Brussels. George and I provided them with clothes, and they stayed at the Lynes for months – the young man got into a munitions factory. Churches lent their schoolrooms for the poor things. Harold Scales got his tennis club to furnish a house a man lent – and we sent a lot of furniture to that. There, families lived in separate rooms. In some places (Blackheath for one) beautiful houses were furnished beautifully and run by subscriptions like hotels or clubs. Some of the Belgians were delightful visitors and did all they could to give as little trouble as possible to their hosts. Others were appalling. Mr and Mrs Glendinning, in Stormont Road, had a Countess, her daughter and grandchild. The Countess used to go up to town, buy handsome clothes and have the bills sent in to Mr Glendinning – she went everywhere in taxis, and they said she needed a retinue of servants. At last they told the Aldwych Committee they could keep her no longer – and Aldwych told her that if she did not behave properly, she would have to go to the Alexandra Palace. (There were some thousands of the very poorest Belgians there.)

We thought we would take 2 Belgian ladies, and we heard of 2 whom we thought would do, but they insisted upon being invited 'for the duration of the war', and that we felt impossible. Then, through Mr Webb of Crescent Road who spends his time looking after the Belgians, we heard of a mother and daughter in a Belgian refugee house in Hornsey and we went to see them. The poor old mother had only one leg and could only speak Flemish. Her daughter spoke French. They seemed very glad to come to us. We gave them the bachelors' room with 2 beds in it, and the morning room. We had them in to meals with us sometimes. I liked Mademoiselle very much and George tried to learn Flemish to talk to the little old lady and she laughed. They only stayed about a fortnight with us as the whole family had a house offered them to live together at Reigate. Their name was Gervais and they came from Antwerp.

The Norman Sargants had a Mr van der Craen, a huge man of about 30. We thought he should have joined the Belgian army and would not have cared to have had him.

On November 28th 1914, a Mme Massey and her son came to see if we could help them. They were sent by the Wanstead cousins. Mr Massey was reckoned in Belgium as a British subject because his father was a Scotsman, but he had died when he was a baby. If he had remained in Belgium he would have been interned in Germany, and one evening they heard that the Germans were coming for him and he and his wife escaped early the next morning in a snow storm. They drove for many miles and just managed to get over the frontier in time. Their son, Raymond, was in England. Monsieur had found work to do with an English committee in Rotterdam – sending over refugees to England from Holland, so she was alone, as her son was provided for. She looked a nice little thing and very sad, so we arranged for her to come to us and she was with us for 3 or 4 months. We liked her very much, but she was very inert and slow and neither read nor worked and she learnt no English. So at last I felt as if we must have the house to ourselves again, and we paid 10/6 a week for her at Miss Dorey's. Monsieur paid 10/6- and Aldwych 10/6-. Last Christmas, 1915, M. Massey said he was able to bear all the expense. He and his son spent the first Christmas here. He is a tall energetic man with auburn hair, and Raymond is a nice boy. He has now gone into the English army and Madame still at Miss Dorey's. It is very sad for her being so long exiled.

The only thing she could say after many months was 'poke ze fire', which was of no great service in summertime.

Christmas 1914 we spent at Blackheath as usual. We gave no presents to each other – by arrangement – nor last Christmas either. Geoffrey Savage was with us the first Christmas as the HAC was quartered at Blackheath. We left the Masseys here, and they ate nearly the whole breast of a large turkey on Christmas Day. Belgians are very fond of meat and do not care for puddings. Ms Massey gave me two little pictures and Raymond a large box of chocolates which I thought very nice of them.

1914. The year ended very darkly. Germans at Antwerp and Ostend, but their advance on Calais stayed. Our loss at the Battle of the Falkland Isles, and on December 14th there was the wicked bombardment of Scarborough, an unfortified town, which roused the most intense indignation through the country. Constance Raynor [school friend of Lillie's] was in her bathroom about 7.30 in the morning when suddenly there was a terrific noise which she thought was our own ships firing close to the shore, but the maids came hammering at the door. She dressed as quickly as possible. Poor Mr and Mrs Raynor were terribly upset – they are so old, but they and the maids were very brave. A shot went through the roof of their house, and in the same road as their house, at their friend Mr Turner's, the maid and postman were both killed at the front door. The cannonading went on for about half an hour. The Raynors got their car to leave the town and Con went to see if Miss Townsly would go with them, and passed houses with the fronts all gone and all the house laid open to the view. They went to Con's cottage 17 miles inland and then later to Harrogate, where they stayed some months. They still have submarine and Zeppelin alarms at Scarborough and hear firing sometimes so Con cannot leave her father and mother for a holiday.

Every disaster only made the nation more determined. Many men too old to join the army – or prevented in some way – joined the National Guard. Bernard joined the Baltic, Harold and Alfred Nutter the Inns of Court. Bernard is now a corporal. The uniform is grey, with a red band with GR on it on the arm. Bernard also does 12 hours' munition work at Woolwich every Sunday. Harold does munition work in the City, and also works at one of the War Office Red Cross depots making splints. These houses are everywhere now, properly organised, under competent women, and each depot has several hundred ladies making bandages, swabs, slippers, bed jackets etc. for the hospitals. Ethel went through first aid and home nursing and got maximum marks for the first. She goes every afternoon to the Lewisham hospital on monthly shifts – works in canteens, and is very busy. Honor Matthews has given up all her time to work among the soldiers and is now doing canteen work in France. Maud has worked for a year at the Khaki Club on the heath – cooking and cleaning rooms – and done canteen work at Woolwich. The VADs are being <u>most</u> useful and I know numbers of girls at work.

We hoped that the war might bring the nation back to God but it has not done so yet. In fact, congregations are smaller than they used to be – partly owing, no doubt, to the men being away, and partly that people have not the heart to take much interest in things, and unfortunately they do not seem to look upon the Church as a refuge. More may be going on between themselves and God than we know though, and one cannot be too thankful that England was brave enough to make a stand for honour and truth, and we know <u>now</u> how brave she was. Everyone recognises that it is a war between ideals – Germany's ideal 'might', England's 'honour'. We have heard many things that have greatly surprised us of the feeling in Germany towards the English before the war and the way in which, for a generation, they have been taught to hate England, and that Germany is supreme because of her 'kultur', and because of her strength. Mr Palliser Young, whose boys were at school in Germany, told us how for an hour every day the German boys were taken privately in classes, and one of his sons found that they were being taught things about other nations and their duties as citizens, and his boys were taught that Germans were the only people who had invented anything and all history was twisted in the most barefaced way to the advantage of Germany. They were deliberately taught that might is right, that many boys might (and did) set on one, in order to win – that they might scratch, kick or do anything to <u>win</u>. Miss Löwenstein told me of a German friend of hers who had been brought to God in England, and of how changed the Bible was to her.

Miss Löwenstein asked her if she had ever read the Bible before, and she said she had read parts of it, for instance, the Beatitudes, but she said, 'We thought it was so <u>silly</u>, we used to laugh and laugh,' and I have seen in the papers a German version of the Beatitude: 'Blessed are they that hate, blessed are the strong' etc. There is no doubt they have thrown over the religion of the New Testament as a nation. It has been an organised system of religious and moral education and we believe that this has made it possible for Satan to enter and take possession. While in spite of her many sins England does still stand for the teaching of Christ, for honour, truth and mercy. And the Kingdom of God <u>must</u> triumph. Therefore we believe that we shall triumph eventually, though God has many things to teach us yet. Admiral Beatty writes in the papers that the war will end when the nation returns to God. God grant that the nation may return to Him, and help us to fight evil for Him, and do what he wants us to do in this matter.

Perhaps the Anglican Mission of Repentance and Hope which is to begin in October 1916 may have great spiritual success.

There has been great drinking among women. They have such good separation allowances that they have money to spend. Some friends of mine took a house in Holloway and called it the 'Cosy Corner Club'. I went to help sometimes, but often that would be 6 ladies to 8 women, so I gave it up, because I was not able to really work at it properly, and I thought I could work better through my class. A 'league of honour' was started for women, and a number of my women joined. They promised to drink no alcohol while the war lasts, and to pray every day, but I don't think it has been a great success. Sister Francis got up a great tea for mothers and wives of soldiers and 300 were invited. A number came and Colin Roberts addressed them very well, and I got a number of their addresses and then was ill and could not do much.

All churches hold Intercession services weekly or oftener. At first they were well attended, but all say they are sagging now.

In some parts of London the poor people make 'shrines' in the streets. They put up the names of all who have gone from that street to the war, their photographs, and vases of fresh flowers. The church will give the vases and the table – the people do the rest.

Miss Löwenstein also told us, and we have heard from other sources as well, of the extraordinary German 'geography'. An American lady, a friend of hers, was living in Germany for a time, and sent her little girl to school. She came home one day and said the girls said she must be a red Indian. In their geography books America was painted pink, with a black streak across it, and some brown colour up in a corner. The black represented the negroes, the brown red Indians, and the pink was 'German' (influence). Therefore being neither black nor German, she must be red Indian! Holland, Denmark etc. were all pink: 'sphere of German influence'.

There were all kinds of little indications of the German feeling towards us if only we had taken them seriously, but we never did. Hatred and war seemed impossible. For instance, there was a girl the cousins knew staying at Wanstead. She came down to breakfast one morning (before the war) and said she had had a lovely dream – she thought the German guns were firing on London, and setting it all ablaze! Another girl wrote in her letter

'We are glad your King Edward has died. He was no friend to us.'

At the beginning of the war, houses were opened everywhere for hospitals. In Crouch End, an empty house was taken, prepared by ladies and beautifully fitted up, but never used, and closed in a few months. Now, however, there are hundreds of these hospitals. There are several in Crouch End. They are presided over by a 'commandant' – lady in charge – there are a few trained nurses and then VADs and the cooking is done by ladies. The soldiers are taken drives by people in their cars and entertained in their houses. Ladies supply cake etc. for their teas at the hospitals.

Zeppelin Raids
An aeroplane came, or tried to come, up the Thames on Christmas Day 1914, but without success, and we quite expected Zeppelin raids. Guns were placed in different parts of London. The nearest to us is at Finsbury Park, and there are a number of guns at the Grand Duke Michael's in Hampstead Lane, which are rushed onto Hampstead Heath and other places when a raid is expected, in great motor lorries. Now, it is wonderful to see the search lights over London. They always work for about half an hour just after twilight, and Millicent Berry counted 37 from her window the other day. They are tremendously powerful. There are 2 on Blackheath, and 2 great guns, and last summer after there had been 2 or 3 raids the

poor people from Greenwich and Deptford used to come and sleep on the heath in great numbers, feeling, I suppose, safe near the guns. Alfred Nutter works on the guns, and Mr Coxon worked on the search lights till he went abroad as Chaplain. He said it was so strange to be on the watch over London at night. You saw such strange unaccountable lights.

Our first experience of a raid was on Tuesday, August 17th 1915. We had been spending the evening at Wanstead and as they had no timetable, we had 20 minutes to wait at Leytonstone Station. The station is high and we noticed how black the night was. There had been a raid a few weeks before, and all gas lamps in London were blacked and shop windows and house windows darkened with shaded lights and heavy curtains. The penalty is very heavy for a naked light. Many gas lamps in the street are turned out altogether and the roads are as black as pitch. You cannot see the edges of the pavement, and you knock into people. Many people carry little electric flashlights, but in some neighbourhoods these are not allowed. The streets are really dangerous and it is said that there have been more accidents through the darkened streets than through Zeppelins. We have known of several personally.

Well, it was a very dark night and we took the 9.52 train. 12 minutes later, just as we were coming up Hornsey Rise, we heard several muffled bangs, and saw curious flashes of light. People ran out of their houses. I thought of guns, but not of bombs, but the next morning we heard that we had <u>just missed</u> a dreadful raid at Leyton. It is thought that the Germans either thought they had got to London, or else they were aiming for the Enfield small arms factory. We went the following Saturday to see the damage done. All the glass of Leyton station was broken, and streets of houses had all the glass of the windows smashed, but it was very extraordinary in how many instances the bombs themselves had fallen in the road, or in yards. Many fell on Wanstead flats. Not many lives were lost. We saw a hole made by a bomb large enough for a cart to go in it. We only missed it by 10 minutes.

September 8th was our next experience. There was a raid on the 7th but we heard nothing of it. I am so used to the noise of the trains and George is deaf. On September 8th, George had gone to bed early with a bad cold and I was in the bathroom about 10.45 when I heard bombs. I thought I had plenty of time to finish my bath, but in a few seconds the noises seemed to be all round the house. I hurried into a bath gown and dressing gown, shouted at the maids to hurry down. They were getting up, unloosed Mac and roused George with difficulty. He could not hear, and hardly thought it was worth getting up for. We made a weird procession into the basement, putting out all the lights, and we opened the tradesman's and kitchen garden door so that we could get out if necessary, and there we stood for a quarter of an hour. It sounded as if things were dropping in the garden and there was shrapnel from our own guns in the lane. After it was over, Harold came down in his dressing gown to see if we were all right. He and Flo had watched the Zeppelin from outside. It looked like a great silver fish or cigar in the sky, picked up by the search lights. Then it suddenly seemed to make for their house and they rushed in, followed by a strange man shaking with fear. Norman Sargant was watching it from his bedroom window and saw it make for his house. He rushed at his wife, picked her up out of bed, and carried her downstairs. Everyone was under the impression that it had gone over their house. Bombs were dropped in Greenwich Park, none of which exploded, but they had had a very alarming time with the big gun so near.

I went up to Morley's Hotel and fetched Millicent Berry home next day. All the people had been hurried into the cellar. Millicent was in a most becoming but very cold and flimsy silk wrapper. They seemed in the very centre of it all, and there noise was dreadful. They could see the fire in Wood Street, and saw the fire engines rushing by and the ambulances. The damage done in Bartholomew's Close was terrible – whole fronts of houses fallen out, but here again the bombs fell in the square, and the hospital, and St Bartholomew's church, were untouched. A bomb fell near a theatre [Lyceum] which was just emptying, and no harm was done, and within a few yards of the post office and Bank of England – I forget which. It is very wonderful.

On Wednesday, October 13th 1915 I heard that Millicent had returned to town, so telephoned to her to come out to us, in case there should be a raid. She came, and Aunt Becca was also with us. At 9.30, Aunt Becca having just gone to bed, we heard bombs or guns and this time saw the Zepp. It was just a line of lights above the trees in the lane and shells were bursting all round it, some near it, and others not at all near. It was a wonderful sight. We went to bed at the usual time and I did not put my coat and shoes ready as I generally did, for I never thought of a second raid the same night. However, at 12 Dorothy came knocking at our door and there was another one on. I ran into Aunt Becca and got her into a dressing gown. She was very shaky. George took her downstairs while I put on a coat and then I remembered Millicent! She was asleep, and would insist on strapping her garter with her money in it round her leg. She took so long that by the time we got into the lower hall the raid was over! When Aunt Becca got into bed again she said, 'If the Zeppelins come again, I shall not rise,' and the next morning she said she had not had such a good night for a long time, and that an exciting night suited her, for she did not know when she had so much enjoyed her breakfast and she is a game old lady.

However, at the beginning of the year, 1916, there was bad raid near Beeston. Aunt Prilla woke up and thought burglars were in the house, knocking Aunt Becca about (she is very deaf). She got into Aunt Becca's room and found her lying peacefully in bed. She said, 'Oh my dear, what is it' and Aunt Becca said, 'It is only those Germans dropping their bombs. Go back to bed again. God is with us.' But the next day Aunt Prilla was ill and she never recovered, dying some weeks later at the age of 85, followed a few weeks later by Aunt Becca at the age of 80. There is no doubt that that raid shortened their lives. The shock of those raids for elderly people is very great. Father and Mother have been sleeping in the morning room at Brathay for a year now (this is written September 1916) as Mother could not get downstairs quickly. The big guns on the heath make so much noise that a raid is very alarming for them (these guns were removed about October 1916 and no one knows why). George and I were there on April 25th 1916 and nurse came knocking at our door about 12.30 to say the guns were beginning. We hurried down to Father and Mother, and they were very calm. We all, with the maids, went and sat in the kitchen which was quite warm. Nurse was most anxious that Mother should sit in the coal cellar! There were no bombs dropped that night anywhere near us. Last Thursday week, August 24th there was a dreadful raid at Blackheath. A house in the village was reduced to dust and wooden splinters, and in the middle of it a brass bedstead was sticking up. An old lady had been killed. The windows of about 30 houses and shops were blown out. Another bomb fell on the heath, and soldiers were injured, and another near Greenwich station. Poor Maud was greatly alarmed, and she says she spent the night in the road talking to the next door coachman and gardener. They (she and Harold) are now staying at Brathay. The search lights over London are wonderful. Just when it gets dark they play for half an hour. I should think more than 200 of them, from all directions, and immensely powerful. We do not seem to be able to tackle these Zepps adequately yet. After the last raid Raymond Massey told me he had seen an English one going over his camp early in the morning, but it is very likely just an imagination of his.

The most extraordinary tales get about. Millicent Berry came in on Monday night to say that Miss Pearse had heard from a friend of hers at Portsmouth that there had been a great naval battle. We had lost 16 ships and the German navy was wiped out. There is not a word of truth in it, and this is a sample of the things one is continually hearing.

Sept 2nd 1916. I wrote this about the Zeppelins last evening. In the night we had another raid. I was awakened by the guns, called the maids and we went downstairs. It was 2.15 in the morning. This morning, I rang Brathay up and Harold said that as he was standing in the front garden, a great glow illuminated the sky and then he saw slowly descending a great ball of fire. Soon we heard of others who had seen it and it was a Zeppelin brought down at Cuffley. [It was shot down by a plane and the pilot got the VC.]

1915. The year 1915 was a very depressing year. On the West both Germans and English settled down to trench warfare. On September 25th we made, in conjunction with the French, a great effort to break the German line. We captured Loos, and made progress at Houge, but it was at great cost and we were not able to follow up our advantage. We were at Bexhill when we heard the news and were full of high hopes.

On April 25th, our men made their wonderful landing on Gallipoli, but all the news about Gallipoli, though it made one thrill with pride at the great deeds of our wonderful men, filled one with terrible forebodings, for George had been to a lecture at the Royal Geographical Society, on Gallipoli, by Professor Hogarth, and he always was convinced that it was impossible country for warfare, as it has been proved. It seems as if those in authority knew much less about this country than Hogarth. I need not write of the muddles and inefficient generalship – that is all a matter of history now – nor of Winston Churchill's bombastic prophesies. We could hardly bear to read the news in the papers, and it was popularly thought that the withdrawal of the army was impossible, that it would be annihilated in the doing, and it was with the greatest relief and thankfulness that we heard of the evacuation of Gallipoli on the January 9th 1916.

We have talked with several Australians who were there. Reginald Dunn described his landing to us. It was to have taken place at night, but it took so long to land the impedimentia that the men did not begin to disembark until daylight. They were in full view of the Turks with their heavy artillery. The colonel seemed quite to lose his head. He crowded them in to the boats and sent them off, and none of them expected to reach the shore. But, providentially, a terrific storm of rain came on which hid them from the Turks and they landed safely. Dallas Taylor, a New Zealander, described how his regiment was to join up with the forces landed at Suvla Bay. How they climbed what seemed to be impossible heights and hung on there for 2 days, waiting for the men from Suvla Bay who were 2 days late, and they had to retire, and the great chance was lost. This is one of the mysteries of the war. He said that the matter was hushed up, because it was the fault of the Duke of Westminster and the Marquis of Breadalbane! He also said that the troops sent out from England were London ones composed of men unused to climbing! And they could not do what they were set to do.

On October 6th 1915, the Allied forces landed at Salonika on the invitation of the Greek government, and there they have been ever since. The political reason we shall probably see later. People give all sorts of reasons for them being there, and now that Roumania has joined the Allies [August 1916] they say that the end is gained.

It is sad to think that there was a time when the Dardanelles were undefended and we could just have taken them, but we waited and gave the Turks a month in which to bring up their armies and entrench. We had the troops ready in Egypt, but their training was not quite complete, I believe.

All the year the news from the colonies was good, which was encouraging. All the German colonies were taken except German East Africa. Hamilton is in British East Africa. Russian news was very variable, sometimes great victories, sometimes great defeats, but the year ended badly in the Bulgarians overrunning Serbia, and the Germans having possession of Poland, and their armies well advanced into Russia.

On May 7th [1915], the *Lusitania* was sunk and all Germany rejoiced and England was wild. Our men rushed into battle shouting, 'Remember the *Lusitania*', our God must punish such cold blooded cruelty. This was followed by the sinking of other passenger ships and Red Cross ships. Mrs Rowley writing to me in December 1915 told me how she and Mr Rowley had worn lifebelts for days in the Mediterranean, and no one took off their clothes. Once they saw the track of a submarine and at

Port Said they took onboard many of the passengers from the *Persia* which had left England a day before they had, and on which they had meant to travel. She was torpedoed, and her passengers had had a terrible experience in open boats. Mr and Mrs Lockwood went through the Suez Canal after a battle and saw the bodies of the Turks lying about.

But it is most wonderful what our navy has done. The way in which it has caught in all sorts of ways the submarines is known now, so I will not write about it.

Last week [24 August 1916] the Germans went nearly mad rejoicing over the arrival of their submarine, the *Deutschland*, with cargo from America. Mr Geddes, who was here, said that it really was the most absolute proof of the supremacy of the British navy that the Germans could rejoice or find anything to rejoice at in the fact that one boat had managed to get from America to Germany, and that it had had to crawl out from under the sea.

At the beginning of the war, we had our 3 cruisers torpedoed, 2 of them going to the help of the other one [22 September 1914: *Aboukir*, *Hogue* and *Cressy*, sunk by one U-boat]. Then there was the naval battle off the Falklands [8 December 1914], and the gradual extermination of the enemies' cruisers who were roaming the seas. Then the naval battle off the Dogger Bank [24 January 1915], after which the German fleet shut itself up and was afraid to come out. We did not hear of it again practically until June 4th 1916.

(February 5th 1917. I have just found this book having lost it for several months.)

1916 [31 May, Battle of Jutland]. I was staying at Wanstead, and when I came down to prayers on Saturday morning, Gertrude and Jessie were looking awful, and Gertrude said, 'The Germans have had a great naval victory in the North Sea.' I shall never forget it. One thought of one's brave men and splendid ships, and of our country, and how our fleet stands between us and Germany. There in the paper were the names of ship after ship that had been sunk, and so few German ships. On Monday the papers spoke quite differently – telling of numbers of German ships sunk, and that our strategy has been most wonderful, and that the German fleet would have been annihilated if a fog had not come on, and the day closed in before we had had time to reap the fruits of our victory, for it was a victory, the German fleet scuttling off for all it was worth and leaving us masters of the sea. Our fleet swept up and down hunting for the Germans, without success.

(Jan. 1922. They never dared to come out again until in solemn procession to surrender. Was there ever such a shameful history of a great fleet?)

On Sunday [4 June], Geoffrey Keble White came to lunch. He is a lieutenant on a destroyer (now he is on a submarine). He took a gloomy view of the situation. Of course the battle was then supposed to be a defeat for us and he said that the navy was so terribly hampered in its movements by civilians at headquarters. He put the 'defeat' down to that, but the news on Monday proved him wrong. It was simply the fog, and the daylight failing. The stories of the heroism of our men – from Admiral Hood downwards, are thrilling. Surely mighty deeds like these must 'exalt' the nation.

The truth about the war in the West is that all that year [1915] we were only marking time and holding our own. I suppose it was not until the failure of our great effort in September 1915 that our authorities realised the immense thing we were up against, and the ammunition and guns we should need. In 1916 Lloyd George was made Minister of Munitions, a new office, and the way in which he took matters in hand was wonderful, and a matter of history. Now there are many hundred, there may even be thousands, of munition factories. Lloyd George used to be our pet abomination, but he is the man now whom everyone turns to, and feels confident in, whether as Chancellor of the Exchequer, Minister of Munitions, settler of trade disputes and now [1917] Prime Minister. He who used to inveigh against the idle useless rich and aristocracy, now sees the aristocracy freely shedding its blood and doing its all for the country, while he had to go down to South Wales to implore 200,000 miners – who said they would as soon have the Kaiser as King George over them – to remember their brothers laying down their lives for them and that they, through refusing to work, were responsible for the lives of thousands. I think his point of view must have changed.

It is now said we can make all the munitions we need, and it is to be hoped we can, for today's paper [5 February 1917] says that America has broken off diplomatic relations with Germany and that Count Bernstoff has received his papers. One is surprised, on the whole. I think everyone had practically come to the conclusion that nothing would make America fight. Mr Adlard was here to lunch today, and he and George think that it is very possible that Germany may now say, 'You see the whole world is against me. I cannot go on.' There seems little doubt that she is on the verge of starvation – unless this is only a trick for a political end, and is very possible. She made the same statement about being on the verge of starvation about a couple of years ago when she thought she could work on America's feelings. I myself think it is more likely that she knows America cannot do her much harm in any case. That she hopes also to bring Holland and Denmark in – then she will overrun them, get a much larger seaboard and is hoping to starve us out by her submarine policy. This last is a very serious thing for us. She has declared that from February 1st she will sink all ships – even neutrals and hospital ships – at sight. She is Satan incarnate. We do not know what this may mean to us, but yesterday, February 4th, Lord Devonport put the nation on its honour about food. He says for each person 3 lbs of flour, 2½ lbs of meat (including breakfast meat) and ¾ lb of sugar must suffice. I find that in our household of 5 we eat about 14 lbs of flour a week in bread, so there is about a pound left for cakes, pastry and biscuits etc. We eat 8½ loaves of bread a week which leaves us 2¼ lbs of flour. Fortunately fish and eggs are not included in 'meat'. We mean to keep within these regulations, but I am sure many won't even attempt it, and it will be difficult. The maids in many houses are a great trouble about the food, but mine are quite all right, and I believe are taking a patriotic view of the whole matter.

The war has touched many of us very little, and now is an opportunity for men and women who can't work for the country much to show what they can do by abstinence. (I read in the paper the other day that it is only domestic servants and munitions workers who eat butter now. The rest of the people eat margarine. This is not quite true! But it contains a germ of truth.) The wages the munition workers and government clerks are getting is out of all proportion to their worth, and the public money is being squandered in a wicked way. There is a little girl, aged 15, at George's office – just left school; she came to him last week and told him she could get 26/- a week in government employ! Mother's parlour maid, a most unreliable girl, has just gone to

Woolwich and has at once been made forewoman of some workroom at 35/- a week! My Harold is now a paymaster at Woolwich. For these posts they only take gentlemen. He works from 9 to 7 for £200 a year. The fact is, the gentlemen will do their work from patriotism, but they must entice the lower classes by high rate of pay.

We were anxious whether Harold could stand these long hours, and so far it has meant all Saturday and Sunday also often, but he seems very well. The office is a great corrugated iron building with a wooden floor and heating store which he is quite near, and there is an excellent canteen quite close where the paymasters have a table to themselves and he has a splendid lunch for a shilling – hot joint, vegetables and pudding. Very different to restaurant prices in London now. A boiled egg now costs 5*d*, a cup of coffee [?], and they won't leave the sugar with you, but if you wish for sugar, allow you to take one piece. (I wonder if people have pocketed the sugar!) It is very difficult now to get sugar. When I was keeping house at Blackheath for Mother, I had the greatest difficulty in getting it. A grocer is supposed to sell a pound of sugar for each 2/- spent with him. Mother's grocer's bills average nearly £2 a week, and yet I could not get sugar. The man declared he had none and then I found from himself that he had been selling to other people, and not sending any to us. Our grocer has treated us very well, but I don't know how we shall manage on ¾ lb a week each! (We find we can manage on less.) Numbers of people have stored sugar but it does not seem a patriotic thing to do, and one feels very angry that they are using so much sugar and corn for beer, on which no limit is set. It is said that the Government is frightened to act drastically in this matter.

The prices which we are paying now for some things are interesting. Beef and mutton: I pay 1/6 a lb, but many people pay 1/8 and 1/10. Pork about the same. Bacon 1/7 to 1/10 (now 2/-). Bread 10¾ a quarter. Sugar 6*d* and 7*d* a lb. Tea 2/4, coffee, eggs (cooking) 3*d* to 4*d* each, new-laid more. Brussels sprouts 4*d* and 5*d* a lb, cauliflower 10*d*, fowls of decent size 5/- to 7/-. Fish: cod even 1/2 a lb (often 1/6 to 1/8), plaice 1/6 to 1/8. These prices make it very difficult for people whose salaries or income have not increased. We pay Street now 6/- a day and he works 4 days for us and we let him have the other 2 to earn extra money in, and he comes in morning and evening to look at the fires in the greenhouses, and we give him a shilling a day for that. Coal is so dear and scarce too, that we are only just keeping enough heat to keep the plants alive. It seems such a pity to let them be killed, and we try to keep only the kitchen fire and one other going. We have to have fires sometimes in the drawing room and library because of the piano and organ and the books, but then we always let out the dining room fire, and picnic in the other room the rest of the day. Wood is very dear too. You hardly get any for 6*d*. Matches are very dear and very bad. All train travelling too is increased 50%. I often go to Blackheath now by bus, which really does not take much longer, especially now that there are fewer trains, and you often have to wait a long time at London Bridge.

I have tried since the war began to be very economical in my clothes. I have not bought stockings or petticoats since the war began – only 2 pairs of suede gloves which are still quite good. I have had to buy one warm pair, and 3 or 4 white washing leather ones. My winter coat is 4 winters old now, but fortunately with a little alteration the last 2 years it looks most remarkably up-to-date (it is a pony cloth with large fur collar and round the bottom black). There are no parties now, so one evening dress is all I have wanted, and that I had remade from an old one. The first 2 years I went to a dressmaker I knew for a silk dress, but they never looked smart or well cut and were (are) a great trial to me to wear (they seem as if they never will wear out, and because of the war I <u>will</u> wear them out) so last year I got a very nice dark bottle green taffeta at Harrods with a copper coloured sash, and gold lace and chiffon on the bodice and I quite believe it will do for a best dress for 2 years. My black fox furs had got very shabby so I had them remade and they will look quite nice for another couple of years. We have not bought a single new thing for the house. Lampshades even I have made out of silk that I had, and we badly need to do some decorating now, but we don't mean to. All the money we can spare goes into the war loan (or to foreign missions!). The one thing that I personally feel I have been extravagant in, is in having a new little dog, a tiny Yorkshire Terrier. But since my heart has gone wrong I have to be in so much, and things sometimes are so depressing, that it is very nice to have a little bright thing about. He cost 20/- but he does not cost much to feed and George is so busy now with meetings he is almost always out. He has been asked to speak several times at meetings for the campaign for 'Spiritual Advance' which is our method of trying to revive spiritual life in our church and people, and I and he are so very glad that he can have any share in it.

I do not know if the churches' 'Mission of Repentance and Hope' has been a disappointment or not, but it has been a great movement, and the results of great movements are seen slowly. I have been to church more than to chapel the last few months, as the doctor does not want me to go to chapel lest I shall get drawn into work again too soon and it has seemed to me that the clergy themselves have wonderfully risen to the great day. I was at Bournemouth when 'The Messenger', Rev. le Fleming, from Ryde came and the services were beautiful.

February 18th, 1917. I must return to my visit to Wanstead in June 1916. On the 3rd we had the news of the battle of Jutland, and on the 5th a lady came in in the afternoon and said she had heard that Lord

Kitchener had been drowned at sea. She was followed by 2 or 3 others telling of the same rumour, but in the evening it was contradicted, only to be confirmed the next morning. We felt it <u>could</u> not be true, it was too awful. Lord Kitchener was <u>the</u> man by whom everyone swore and whom everyone trusted. He had done such wonderful things for the nation and it hardly seemed as if a greater disaster could have happened to us. And for it to happen in the way it did. Everyone cried 'treachery'. It seemed as if we were having blow on blow. In April there had been the Irish rebellion and there was still great disaffection in parts of Ireland. We heard privately a great deal more than was in the papers – how officers were sniped as they went into side streets etc. and in June we were terribly afraid that Verdun would fall.

Geoffrey Keble White, that day he came to Wanstead, said it was sure to fall, but on July 1st our great offensive began and continued steadily until the early setting in of rain in the autumn stopped it. Autumn set in so early last year and the mud on the Somme front was too shocking for words. The shelling had been so terrible that the ground already was in a dreadful state. Men frequently sank in it to their waists and even their necks, and often have to leave their great boots which reach up to their thighs in the mud. We have had some terrible descriptions of the Somme offensive. Howard Savage was killed on the first day. Bertram told me that he felt sure he should be killed that day, and he dressed himself in his best suit got at a very smart tailors in Bond Street, and took his little cane. He had been given the roughest platoon in the regiment, and he had got the men into shape, and they adored him and would have followed him anywhere.

He had been through the African campaign after De Wet and was a splendid young fellow – jolly, sweet tempered and as pleasant and gentle and quite the favourite nephew of the family. He was 30 years old. George's cousin, Geoffrey Cather, was killed about the same time, bringing in wounded, and he got the Victoria Cross. That July 1st was a terrible day.

September 15th and 23rd were also very bad. Leonard Bottoms was here to dinner last Sunday [February 1917] and told us some ghastly stories. He told us about the tanks. He said when they first started, they only went over the rough ground at the rate of about 2 miles an hour. The average pace of the infantry in attacking is 4–6 miles an hour, and the German guns got the exact range of the supporting infantry and practically wiped it out. But he says the tanks are wonderful and will go over everything. In the charge on September 23rd – in George Bottoms' company – the Major was killed. The Captain took his place – he was killed. The 1st Lieutenant took his place, he was killed. The 2nd Lieutenant took his place, and still the men went on. George Bottoms took his place. He was shot across the face. The Sergeant took his place. He was shot in the arm, but they got their objective!

The same day Leonard was blown, by the force of an explosion from a shell, 500 yards – alighted on his head and was in hospital a month. He told us that some of the officers when they first go out are very new and want to take the men where it is not well to take them, and rather than lose their own lives the men shoot them. He himself saw Major General or Brigade General Cooke (?) killed. He wanted the men to follow him over the parapet and they would not. He told them he should shoot them if they did not come, and he shot 3 with his pistol and then someone shot him. One hears these things of the Germans, but it is dreadful to hear them of one's own men.

He told us of a curious meeting he had had with George. He and George were separated to their great grief. One night Leonard was on a road which was often fired on by the enemy and he was told off to warn our troops to go over this part of the road in single file, and carefully. He heard and saw a lot of men marching along 4 abreast, whistling and singing, and went to tell them, when at the head of them he saw George walking 'with his old white head'. (His hair is remarkably light.)

Talking of hair reminds me of Bertram. He is over 41 and only just managed to get into the army. He was at a camp 2 miles out of Winchester, and George and I went to spend the Sunday at Winchester to see him. He got us a room at the 'God Begot', a most ancient hostelry in the High Street. The dining room opened straight into the street, and it is a wonderful old place. When Bertram came in, I was not sure if it were he. When I had last seen him he was a very pale man with very grey hair. This was a red man, with brown hair. I could not help laughing, and he said he had used a hair restorer, *not* a dye. He thought his grey hair might impede his progress in the army! Very sporting of him. He was very keen, and very anxious, to get to France, and the beginning of this month, he went – in great spirits. I trust he will come home safely and I feel so grieved for Uncle and Auntie. They are both nearer 80 than 70 and Bertram was the last one at home and everything to Auntie.

March 3rd, 1917. I do this writing in such scraps that I find it difficult to be at all consecutive. When I get up to date I may do better.

On November 3rd, 1916, Cecil Dunn arrived here from Australia. Reginald who is still suffering from his side (consequent on his operation for appendicitis onboard ship being performed with unclean instruments) hoped to meet him here, but he had to leave on the day Cecil arrived. He is such a little chap, only 18, and looks much younger, but he is fearfully keen on getting out, and was afraid lest the war should be over before he got to England. On February 13th, 1917, Reginald came again for 48 hours, hoping to meet his elder brother, Jack, from the Somme, but he has not come yet [3 March] and we hear that all leave is stopped. It is very hard on the boys.

At the end of 1916 the Asquith ministry fell and nearly everyone was <u>glad</u> for everyone felt that more energy was needed and Lloyd George was welcomed as Prime Minister. 5 years ago we should have thought it impossible that our hopes would be centred in him, and now reforms of all kinds are being pressed forward. At present the war has touched people in our class of life wonderfully little, except when those near and dear have gone to the Front, but now it is coming nearer to us.

My Dorothy may volunteer for national service, and I would not keep her back if she is wanted. She has been engaged for 2½ years, and married the end of last year, as her friend had joined the army and was expecting to go to India. However, he has been sent to Yarmouth instead. She remains here, and if she left I should have to get someone to help Alice and Elizabeth or close part of the house. With this rationing it looks as if it will be difficult to have visitors, and if so, there would be less for them to do, and we might manage with the two, though both of them are such delicate girls. It would be all right if they were strong and if I could do what I used to. I have proposed to George to do the gardening! He won't consider it, and it would be queer gardening. The only time he ever tried to cut the lawn he wore his top hat pushing the mower! There is no 'society' visiting now at all. We have a good many people to stay, but they are really mostly visitors consequent on the war in some way or other – Maud and Harold to give them a little change from their hard work, and to get them away from Zep raids, soldiers, Millicent Berry as she cannot get back to Australia, ministers because of meetings held in London as travelling is so difficult now etc., and I should be sorry not to be able to have these.

All of us had very quiet and inexpensive holidays last year. This year it looks as if we might get none, but nothing matters if only the war could end in the right way. At the end of the year came the German 'peace proposals', but no one thought they meant anything, and we would not have peace on their terms. There is no doubt that the war has a very depressing effect. I am sure it has caused my dear father's illness. There is no doubt it has affected both him and Mother very much. It is very sad for old people, and they cannot shake off the gloom even as younger people can, though one always has a sense of trouble and evil hanging over oneself. Theatres are very full, but mostly with soldiers and their friends. There is a super tax of 2*d* in the shilling on all tickets for entertainments. I think I have only been twice since the war began to a theatre.

We have given no Christmas or other presents since the war began and last Christmas was a very sad one – partly through Father and Mother's illness. The streets are so dark that unless the moon is shining you cannot see a thing. Very few lights are lit, and those almost all blacked or greened, and I would not go out at night without my little electric torch. But one never hears a word from anyone about giving in. I don't think it ever occurs to anyone.

1917. I am now going to begin the year 1917 but this is not in any way a history of the war. It is only a putting of a few things which come into my own life which I shall like to read in years to come, for one forgets so easily.

On January 19th, George and I had just sat down to dinner when there was an awful bang. I thought the windows were coming in. We turned out the lights and I opened the front door for there was no further sound. I saw the lights going out in the house opposite, but absolute darkness and nothing else. (We thought it was a Zeppelin bomb in the garden.) Then I knew it was a terrible explosion somewhere, and at once thought of Woolwich, and Harold who might be working in the arsenal, and of the effect on Father and Mother. I rang up on the telephone and could only get the answer 'number engaged'. At last I implored the girl at the exchange to tell me if there had been some dreadful disaster at Woolwich and she said, 'Yes'. All the evening I was trying to get on and could not. George was out and at last Ethel got on to me at 9 o'clock. They had had a dreadful time. She was sitting in the drawing room with Father when there was a terrific noise and a lot of stuff came down the chimney.

They jumped up to go to Mother, and found the door had jammed. However, they got out at last. Mother had kept wonderfully calm.

Glass from the upper windows had crashed down in front of her window, and windows had also been broken below, but happily her windows held. The latch of the side door was wrenched off, and the skylight twisted and windows broken. Ethel ran back to little Joyce who was alone, and then hurried down with one of the maids to Harold's, as they could not get on to them on the telephone. Harold had just got home. He was on a tram, or rather had just got off, when a dreadful lurid light illumined the sky, followed by 2 deafening reports. He heard from a friend afterwards that every woman on the top of the tram fainted and they had the greatest difficulty in getting them down the steps. The general belief in Woolwich and even in Blackheath of people who saw the light was that the end of the world had come. The light was of the most extraordinary description – a strange yellow, followed by deep red. There were 2 explosions. First the high explosives factory at Silvertown, North Woolwich, and then the gasometer which was exploded by some burning thing from the factory falling on it. Everyone said it was such a relief to hear the noise. The light was seen some seconds before the noise was heard. Even over here people walking along the dark streets noticed them suddenly becoming light – that they could see objects in them – and then came the noise.

Maud had a horrid experience. She was looking out of her bedroom window when the trees in Greenwich Park gradually began to become distinct, and this strange light developed. She thought at once of a Zeppelin in flames. And then came the noise. Her large toilet glass swung round out of its frame and all the electric lights went out. 5 women banged at the front door imploring to be let in, and of course she did so.

The shock upset Mother's nerves very much, and now [3 March] she still has to have sleeping draught.

On February 1st the Germans announced their future career of frightfulness with their submarines, and each day when we open the papers we see a list of ships sunk. It is very dreadful, and one thinks of the poor passengers and sailors in open boats this bitter weather, for ever since Christmas the weather has been colder than it has been for 25 years. One wonders they survive at all, and our merchant seamen are heroes. For some weeks now [3 March] no women or children have been allowed to leave England, and it is even very difficult for men to get passports. Mr Geddes has failed to, and Mr Beason over from Australia cannot get back, and we know of other cases. The papers are continually saying how necessary it is to be careful of food, and that there are still many unpatriotic people who are not attempting to ration themselves, and that compulsory rationing will become necessary. It is disgusting of people, but in some cases

– poor people with large families – it is very difficult for them. We can manage quite well, and the larger the family the easier it is, but children need so much bread. Ethel is troubled about Honor at school. The girls' bread has been cut down and nothing put in its place, as might be – such as barley buns or oatcake.

There is no doubt that many submarines are being caught, but we are not told of these. We hear many stories – Mr Parkyn had heard on good authority from Portsmouth that 2 submarines had put in, flying the white flag – and <u>with no officers on board</u>. We hear of others having come into other ports, and George was told that one way of catching them is: when a submarine is sighted, for a destroyer to whirl round and round very quickly over the point it submerged, and this brings it up to the top. This does not sound very credible! We are losing about 16 ships – over 1,000 tons' burden – a week on an average.

March 25th, 1917. Instead of our losses being put in the papers daily, they appear weekly, and so there is not nearly so much talk about them. In fact, submarine warfare is not mentioned much now – one gets so used to things. We had a letter from Miss McDonald yesterday saying how often they heard firing at Eastbourne, and how the lifeboat had often been out, and ships had been sunk at Beachy Head. I should not like to live on the east or south-east coast just now. I had a letter from

Constance Raynor last week. She said she had just been out for a walk when she heard a loud report from the bay. She saw only some white smoke (it was a hazy day) but a girl rushed up to her and said, 'Did you see that ship blown into the air, and break in half?', and it <u>was</u> a ship blown up by a mine. There were 7 survivors.

Percy had rung Constance up the night before urging her to get her parents inland. That a friend of his who is in the motor ambulance (volunteer) told him they had been warned to be in readiness to fetch wounded, and that trams were standing ready to evacuate civilians and bring up the military. It is very agitating for her, especially as she can't move Mr Raynor if she would, but we have known this fact about the trams for a long time, and most, if not all, towns have their orders what roads are to be used for the military and what for the civilians in case of invasion, but one never knows. Bernard says the National Guard has orders to hold themselves ready and trench digging is being pressed forward.

The great excitement the last fortnight has been the German retreat. We have rejoiced, because retreat <u>is</u> a sign of weakness, but we have not taken many prisoners, and it is in no sense a rout. On Saturday, the papers said they were beginning to make a stand again on the Arras–St. Quentin line. They have just been shortening their line. There has been no excitement whatever about this retreat, and I think at the back of most people's minds has been the thought it might be a trap even. After the long great effort, and all the sorrow, it will need a real great victory to excite us.

Kut and Baghdad had fallen, and all seems to be going well with General Maude's expedition, and now the Turks are being driven by the Russians towards us, so another Turkish army may be in peril. Anyway, the war news in the early part of this year is much more satisfactory, and hopeful, than that of the early part of last year, and also the internal and domestic condition of Germany seems very desperate. One hears continually of food riots, and the speeches of the food controllers are very serious. Last Saturday week we met a lady and gentleman at the Norman Sargents who had left Hamburg a month ago. This gentleman is about 60, and has lived there for years, and his money is locked up there or he would have left earlier. However, they were nearly starved, and felt it was better to lose their money than to starve. The lady said that everything the papers said about the food conditions was true. That the shops were literally empty, that she had to be all day going about trying to get food, and what she did get was indigestible stuff that was making them ill – when they got to England, it seemed like 'fairyland'. They had got *The Times* fairly regularly in Hamburg, so knew the conditions in England pretty well.

They had also been able to communicate with their son in England through Holland. They had a son interned at Ruhleben.

The lady said the sleeping conditions there were very bad – 6 in a horsebox – but there was open air life. They had their own captains and governed themselves, and the soldiers were decent, especially if they gave them some of their food. It is the high command that is so atrocious.

There is a general idea that it would not be desirable that Germany should be obliged to give in owing to her economic difficulties – that victory in the field is essential.

One wonders how this submarine warfare will affect us. George's business – Australian merchant and shipper – has ceased. Practically nothing may be exported now, and the restrictions make it impossible and yet it seems a pity, for ships must go to Australia to fetch the wheat etc. Do they go empty? There won't be much money for the next war loan if no business is done. However, I don't suppose they could get the goods if they could ship them. All the trades are being 'combed out' and the import and manufacture of many things is forbidden. Rabbits have saved us financially, and we are most thankful.

At the present time it is almost impossible to get potatoes. This is said to be not owing to submarines, but to the failure of the potato crop all over Europe. Going along in buses you see, in the poorer districts, long queues of poor people by the greengrocers' shops, and only fruit displayed. No vegetables except a few swedes. I do not like to see those queues at all. One fears it may be the beginning of worse days. Bread is to go up to 1/- a quarter tomorrow.

Everyone is advised to plant vegetables, and we are putting as many as we can in our garden. Plots of ground are being let out to people, and wherever you go you see these plots on the wasteland. I saw a lot of boys yesterday employed digging up the lawn in front of a church in Islington. But lots of this ground will be no good unless properly treated, and many of the people who have them have no expert knowledge. Street says that great quantities of seed will be wasted. It ought all to have been properly organised. It has been by some town councils – such as Southend. The land there has been properly ploughed for the people and they have received instruction. Nothing like that has been done here. Harold Scales has a plot in which he digs!

One morning the week before last when we opened the morning paper we saw 'Revolution in Russia. Abdication of the Czar.' We could hardly believe our eyes. The news was a bombshell, though people afterwards said we might have noticed that there had been no Russian news for 5 days. At first, one wondered and felt very anxious as to what effect this would have on the war, but soon one was reassured. I had wondered for some time why the Russians were doing apparently so little, and now it is evident that treachery has been at work. The Empress apparently at its head. One is very sorry for the Czar, and was very grieved yesterday to read of his being in custody. It is too reminiscent of the French Revolution. I am afraid, however, that one is very selfish, and looks at the matter principally from the point of view of the war, and hopes that internal affairs will settle down and that it will be conducted now energetically. Great events now seem only episodes and phases.

George is now going to the Highgate War Depot twice a week to carpenter. All my spare time is taken up now at Blackheath. I go for 3 or 4 days a week. Though we have Nurse Frances and Miss Davies, one of us has always to be there, and sometimes 2 of us while my dear father is in this sad condition, and we may find indeed that we have to have a second nurse, but we shall do without this if possible.

Lately we have had a young Canadian soldier in several times named Silas Wright. He must be 6 feet 3 or 4. He is just 21, and has been wounded so is now working at headquarters. He comes from a Canadian farm, and has 10 brothers and sisters. He showed us his photographs of them, poor boy, and seemed so pleased to talk about his home. He has joined the choir.

March 29th, 1917. Bernard is on guard at the Rotherhithe tunnel tonight. He is sergeant, and has 6 men and a corporal. It is a responsible post, as it is the main route to Woolwich for munitions etc. and Ethel does not at all care about his taking it, but he likes it. Their breakfast

– paid for by the government – is <u>not</u> rationed. Sausages, eggs and bacon, fried in butter at 2/6 a lb.

Dear Father has not recognised anyone since Saturday. The male nurse is a great help and a very nice man. Father has been in bed since Sunday. We were very fortunate to get a man nurse just now. Dear Mother is so sweet and brave, and we have a carrying chair to take her to him in case of any sudden change. Of course, she is downstairs and he is upstairs.

18 British ships over 1,000 tons were torpedoed last week. That is the worst week we have had.

April 13th, 1917. The submarine menace still continues. Last week just about the same number of ships were sunk, but there were more arrivals and departures, which is encouraging, and we have all been greatly thrilled by America's entry into the war. President Wilson made a great speech. Many people say that, though the moral effect will be great, there will not be an appreciable difference made to the war by the Americans joining, but there <u>must</u> be. They are evidently prepared to give great financial aid, which may make an enormous difference. They have already begun to build 1,000 3,000-ton boats and are going to do their best about the submarines. Their navy is to work with us, and if the war continues till next year, which God forbid, they will no doubt help us with men, which might make <u>all</u> the difference.

Brazil, Panama and other South American states are following suit. All are furious at the Germans' treatment of neutral ships. Today there are rumours again of peace overtures by Bulgaria and Austria and Turkey.

(George read that Balfour has gone to America to discuss terms.) April 9th. Bernard brought the news in the evening paper.

Last Monday the great push began. Our splendid men have done wonders. The Vimy Ridge has been taken, Lens is threatened and they are drawing near to St. Quentin. The co-ordination at the Front of the various services is wonderful. As the guns begin their great cannonade our airmen fly out like great black birds, right over the German lines, and signal to the men how to direct the barrage. Walking or running, just behind the barrage come the infantry, almost close upon it and so accurate and wonderful is it sometimes that in the paper today I read that the Springboks had actually got into the Germans' first line without a casualty. They walked behind the curtain of fire as if on parade, each regiment led by its colonel. But the casualty lists are sure to be terrible. Mr Banks has lost his only son.

(Up to the following Friday, 13,000 prisoners and many guns taken.)

It was Reginald Dunn's 21st birthday on Monday. We meant to have had a party – a little one – for him, but Father is so very ill that we could not think of it. He said that he would like Ethel and Bernard and the children and Miss Mallarky to come better than anything, and, as Ethel and I could not both be away from Blackheath, Bernard and Honor and Joyce came. We waited dinner till a quarter to nine, and then had to begin, though neither Reginald nor Miss Mallarky had arrived. Poor Reginald did not turn up till 10.15. A wretched major was 'too busy' to sign his leave, and all the trains were late as it was Easter Monday. He had his dinner in the drawing room, and though it was very disappointing, it was as well he did <u>not</u> come to dinner for Joyce was most awfully sick at the table! A dreadful catastrophe, poor child, and the next morning she had a high temperature, and Ethel fetched her home in a motor car. (She was quite well the next morning!)

As Reg had had such a poor birthday, George took him to the Coliseum on Tuesday afternoon, and he, Honor and I went to see *London Pride* at Wyndham's Theatre in the evening. We did enjoy it. His leave ended on Wednesday and he left at 5.00. It is probably his last leave before going to France. The Anzacs who for the past year have been ill and recuperating in England are now being formed into a division to go abroad. One felt very much saying goodbye to the boy. Cecil has not written to anyone since he went out, except one letter to

me! It is naughty of him, and all his people are greatly
worried but Reginald happened to meet his sergeant
who said he was all right and the bravest little chap.
He is always over in 'no man's land', and volunteers for
everything.

In his letter he said,

> The weapon that causes most discomfort is the 'Minnie'.
> It is flung into the air to the height of 200 feet, then turns,
> and strikes the ground with terrific force, burying itself
> a few feet below the surface of the ground.
>
> Few moments elapse before it explodes. The concussion
> throwing all objects within a radius of 10 feet many feet
> into the air. I happened to be one of the unfortunate
> objects that night, being thrown up against the parapet
> of the trench but after a good sleep I felt right as rain,
> getting off without a scratch.

The sergeant said that a bomb had exploded, burying
a lot of the men, including himself, and Cecil had dug
him out.

April 15th. Yesterday we heard that the hospital ship
Gloucester Castle had been torpedoed without warning
on March 30th. (Rejoiced over by German official
wireless.) All the wounded were successfully removed,
about 450, and the staff. It was a most difficult operation,
but the weather was good. Many of them were lifted on

their stretchers from vessel to vessel. In the same paper was the news that British hospital ship *Salta* had been sunk by a mine. There were no wounded on board, but 5 doctors, 9 nurses and 38 RAMC were drowned.

The *Asturias*, while steaming with all lights and the Red Cross brilliantly illuminated, was sunk without warning on March 20th.

The Germans are demons.

We have had a large piece of our lawn dug up for potatoes, but the weather has been so atrocious that we have not been able to plant yet. It is the worst winter for 80 years. The trees are absolutely bare still, and there has not yet been a day since November when one has not been glad of one's warmest furs. Last week, only, the snow was inches deep. In January and February there were only 7 hours' sunshine in the city. If the sun does get out now, the winds are bitter and this, combined with the war, is making things dearer than ever. Tiny cauliflowers are 8*d*, Brussels sprouts 8*d* a lb, a tiny cabbage 8*d*. No potatoes. Haricot beans now 1/- a lb and sometimes impossible to get. No macaroni, and every day the papers are imploring people to eat less bread. We are to buy barley flour and maize meal, and I tried to get some last week, but only succeeded in getting 1 lb. Cheese is 1/6 a lb, bacon 2/-, milk 6*d* a quart, but one can get plenty of food, and the rations are voluntary. But all honourable people who realise the condition of things are doing their best to keep to them. We are going to try to do with less than our bread rations, and I think we can with management.

Yesterday, we went to see Quinton and Mary. Ronald is a flight observer. Godfrey is on active service in Egypt. Douglas leaves school in the middle of next term and goes into the Flying Corps. I am sorry for Q. and M., though they must be very proud too. Ronald has had extraordinary escapes. Once his pilot was killed while he was on leave, and the other day Ronald was going up and the pilot said he would give his servant a joyride first, and he turned too quickly, set his machine on fire, and both were killed. Poor Mary did hope and think that the war would be over before Douglas was of age to go.

At Mapperley House, we saw Hugh Savage, the last of the 4 brothers to come. He is such a good looking boy. He is now in the RA Cadet School at Regent's Park.

April 21st. Last Thursday week George heard that Mr Balfour had gone to America. Today his arrival is in the papers, and that is the first notice of the matter. Everything is kept very quiet. France's great move began the end of last week, and in 8 days the Allies took 31,000 prisoners, and the advance is still going forward, but there is no excitement here.

People have had so much to bear and have lost so much that there is only thankfulness and grim determination to see it through.

It almost seems as if the British, at any rate, were not going to attempt anything more just at present for leave has started again, and when I got home from Blackheath yesterday evening there was a telephone message from Jack Dunn saying he had arrived in London, and at 7.30 he arrived. He looks younger than Reg and has evidently been through some terrible times. He is in the AAMC. He told us how they used the German trenches as dressing stations and how the Germans left tempting souvenirs about in them: a helmet, field glasses, bottle of wine, and these had wires attached and when the men would naturally pick them up, bombs would explode and blow them up. Now engineers go in first to examine the trenches evacuated. On entering, a heavy step on a wooden step would explode a bomb. When our men entered nearly all the buildings were destroyed except the town hall which was intact and immediately taken possession of by headquarters staff. All went well for 4 days and then there was an awful explosion and many were killed.

The Germans had left a mine which was exploded in the following way. The wire was left in some acid, and when the acid had eaten through the wire, the wire or weight dropped, and exploded the mine. Jack was working right up at the Front in this great push. It took him 2 days to get here, beginning with a walk of 25 miles. He was met at Waterloo by Australians who took him to Horseferry Road, where he got a bath and change before coming here. Today he has gone to Salisbury to see Reg.

Yesterday was America's day, and the King and Queen drove to the service at St Paul's. Coming home from Blackheath it was so curious to see the American flag flying everywhere, with the Union Jack. They looked so gay in the sunshine. I don't remember to have seen it flying before except perhaps once or twice on the Continent. It looked very unfamiliar.

Could get no margarine today! No more fancy cakes or pastry are to be sold and sugar is to be reduced to half a pound a week. It is quite right about cakes. It is absurd to be so careful about bread and to see the shops full of cakes, and does not encourage flour economy. People do their own shopping a great deal now. You meet them with big baskets and the shops are crowded. I hate it. And it is very funny how stout people are getting thin. I met Mrs Hunt's maid, Barrett, today, and hardly knew her. She is so much thinner. Result of rations.

It is said that now America has come into the war, Ireland is in a great difficulty. There is no one to support her either morally or financially.

Great social and political upheavals invariably exercise a certain influence upon the whole commonwealth of nations, and this the Russian Revolution has done. It has been warmly welcomed by the various republics, and there was a silly letter in *The Times* today from H. G. Wells suggesting that 'Republican circles' should be formed to fraternise with the French, Russian and American Republics. *The Times* says clever men only sometimes write foolishly and points out that we are a 'crowned democracy', that our King has less power than President Wilson, our parliament more power than Congress, but that our Monarchy is a golden thread which binds together our vast fabric of empire. It appeals to the great self-governing states beyond the seas. They look upon the King 'as the supreme symbol of unity'. To the Crown Colonies it is the tree under whose majestic shade liberty is sheltered in its growth. To the immense Indian Empire, kingship is by immemorial tradition the very foundation of order and of peace. 'All democracies must mould their own institutions. We have chosen a kingship – founded on the will of the people and ruling by that will.'

April 30th. The following is the copy of a letter I received from Cecil yesterday. I am sending the original on to his mother.

24/4/17
No. 2068 C. Dunn C Comp.
Australian Imperial Forces, France

Dear Mrs Scales

Once again I am indebted to you for the letter and parcel you sent me, a combination which filled me with delight, literally and otherwise. Thank you also for the splendid anniversary Reg received at your hands. What with the weight of 21 years coupled with cuff links of gold he is indeed a man of no mean repute. Mother is very grateful to you for all the kindness shown towards her three laddies. In a letter to me the other day I was asked if I had thanked you properly. I am afraid that the letter that replies to it cannot be in the affirmative.

As for life over here, we are managing very well and now that the ground is hardening and the weather favourable we have hopes of taking part in scattering our stubborn ponderous Fritz, or to put it in his own official way 'We will withdraw back to our own frontier according to strategic plans of General Hindenberg.'

The book is a beauty. I simply revelled in it for two days but of course, like all other books, there was an ending to it but the story just suits my romantic taste perfectly. [It was one of Conan Doyle's detective stories!]

Well I am sure we shall do our best to finish this job, and be in time to join you at an <u>English</u> Christmas dinner.

Yours sincerely

Cecil Dunn

April 30th, 1917. Last Wednesday 40 ships over 1,600 tons were reported as having been torpedoed or mined, and there was a very serious statement by Lord Devonport on the food question. He said that if everyone would do their duty, and strictly economise, there is sufficient food in the country till the harvest, but that the next 6 weeks will be a very critical time. On Friday, Capt. Bathurst said that people were eating flour at the rate of 6 lbs a head a week instead of three as was requested (we are using under three). Very many people <u>are</u> honourably rationing and this must mean that <u>many</u> are unpatriotic pigs. It is said that it is the <u>artisan</u> class that are principally to blame.

The soldiers are being rationed, and one cannot bear that. Bertram wrote home to Quinton, asking him to send him a 4 lb loaf of bread. I sent him a large cake and some scones yesterday, as the bread is so dry. Mrs Arnold wrote that Mr Arnold is 'hungry', and Jack Dunn says that they are allowed one thick slice at each meal. He says you get quite used to it, but he is a boy who makes the best of everything.

He and Reg did not meet until 10 o'clock on Saturday night when Reg found him in his bed in camp. There had been a series of contretemps. On Sunday Reg got leave until Tuesday, being able to produce Jack in the body, and prove that he had a brother just home from the Front, and they arrived here about 9 o'clock having spent the day talking under a hedge, there being no trains to London until the evening. They were so delighted to be together and had a great time the next 2 days. I sewed

Jack's badge of 'once wounded' on his sleeve. He had a piece of shell go through his forehead, just missing his eye and artery!

Tuesday evening Jack spent here, as he wanted to have one evening at home, and 2 New Zealanders came to tea and dinner. He sings very nicely. Wednesday I went with him and George to see St Olave's and St Saviour's Barking, and then he and I went to the Tower, then took the tube to Central Buildings, Westminster to an organ recital by Meale where there must have been 3,000 people nearly, then to lunch at the 'Popular', then I did a little shopping and came home and he went on to Madame Tussauds and Ethel's. They took him to the zoo the next morning and he went to Birmingham in the afternoon returning on Friday evening and meeting George at the Gaiety. They came home in great spirits. Yesterday morning he met George at Westminster Abbey having previously been at the Houses of Parliament, they came home to lunch, and then went to hear 'Hiawatha' at the Albert Hall. Came home to dinner and then he and I went to *Hamlet*. Henry Irving. No scenery, good acting. This morning (Sunday) he is in bed and I am not surprised. But he has spent his time just as he wanted. He leaves London very early on Tuesday morning, and one does feel parting with these boys.

Having dug up the end of our lawn for potatoes, we are now digging up the lower lawn for vegetables. At least, it is pegged out, if George approves. One does not want to reproach oneself next winter for not doing all one could this summer. It is still very chilly, and not even the pear tree is out yet.

April 20th, 1917. Last week there was a most brilliant sea fight [destroyers] when the *Broke* greatly distinguished herself. Also the *Swift* [in Dover Straits against German torpedo boats].

Dear Father still is in the same condition. It has been a dreadful winter, but it might have been much worse.

Last night, coming home from *Hamlet* we passed the long string of motor ambulances waiting for the wounded at Charing Cross. There must have been quite 50.

May 10th. Glorious weather, and no rain for more than 3 weeks. The fruit trees are nearly in full bloom – not quite. Father just the same, to the doctor and nurses' great surprise. Occasionally he seems to recognise us, but we cannot be sure, and we cannot understand most of what he says. The household at Brathay is going on fairly smoothly, for I believe the 5 women there are all good women, and anxious for the comfort of the household in this most trying time, but things are rather funny. The maids all hate Miss Davies, and none of them will do a thing more than what they consider their work. There is no love lost between Miss Davies and Nurse Frances. I believe they are very jealous of each other. Cook has to be treated very tenderly or she would give notice. Lydia is most capable, but always sure she is right. Alice is of a sentimental adoring disposition and worships Nurse.

Nurse and Miss Davies are tremendously capable, and have very strong opinions. Mr Garton is the easiest member of the household, but he won't speak to Miss Davies. He thinks she tries to manage him. Miss D. lays down the law, but she is most reliable. The rationing there is very difficult and they are not keeping quite within either fat flour or meat, but Mother cannot do more than she has done. It is very difficult with such a mixed up lot. I am very thankful for my maids. We manage with one loaf each a week, and have given up all flour puddings. We have two cakes a week, one for upstairs and one down, and we have barley scones or oatcake for tea, but we don't have two-thirds of our ration. I am afraid Ethel is starving herself and family for if you don't have bread you ought to have fish, eggs, milk etc. at any rate while they are plentiful! They cook nettles and say they are very good. Harold and Maud cooked rhubarb leaves, and the next day there was a piece in the paper about cases of poison through rhubarb leaves.

Jack took a day's extra leave, and went back on Wednesday. He said his colonel would not mind at all. The only fear was lest the military police might get him, and as they raid the YMCA huts at night, he spent his last night here, and left at a quarter to seven. Dorothy got up and got his breakfast, and I woke up in good time, for we are all so afraid of oversleeping and that he should miss his train. The poor boy seemed very sad at leaving. He did not say much, but as he sat eating his breakfast he was looking out over the garden which looked lovely in the early morning light, and he suddenly said, 'It's a dreary prospect.' For the moment I thought he meant the garden, and then I understood. One is grieved to the heart for these boys. George went with him to Finsbury Park.

On Sunday, April 30th, Lieutenant Jacobs came to dinner. He was leaving that evening for East Africa. He had been badly wounded in the neck, and was very pleased not to be going back to France. Last Sunday, George and Leonard Bottoms came to dinner. George has come out first of 100 officers and is gazetted to the King's Own Rifles. He asked if he could come again on Tuesday, which he did. They volunteered the first week of the war. George was wounded on September 15th 1916 and of his battalion of 800 less than 100 came out.

He told us how the men advance singly, and an officer cannot keep touch of more than 6 or 7 men because there are spaces between them and there is always smoke. The men are told where to go and they <u>get there</u>! But it is often as if you were advancing quite alone, and it takes great courage. The Germans cannot do it. The utmost they can do, if they do not advance in a solid phalanx, is to go in groups of 10 or 12.

On Monday week, 2 New Zealanders came, Wagg and McAye, on their way to Scotland – three days' leave! And one day last week Mr Jackson turned up on his way to Cambridge to have officers' training. He seemed to have quite recovered, and looked very fit, and is very much in love with his little nurse. On Tuesday, George brought Mr Brooker's son home. He also is taking his officers' course. He has been in France – in King Edward's Horse, a force somewhat resembling a foreign legion. There were men in it from Patagonia, Iceland, Falkland Isles, and every imaginable place – all fine riders. He had been sent to Ireland in the Rebellion, and had had a fine time, riding round. Once they stopped a funeral, and found the coffin full of rifles.

Last Sunday, the King's Proclamation was read in church. The thing one really feels most anxious about now is Russia's attitude. There is talk of her making a separate peace, and one wonders what that would mean. I am afraid there has been terrible fighting going on in the last 10 days. The Germans are standing and counter-attacking at Fresnay and Bullecourt.

On Tuesday, May 1st, Jack and I went to see the Maha Rajah, General Smuts and 3 others receive the freedom of the city. The Guild Hall looked beautiful with the sun streaming in and the scarlet and blue robes of Aldermen and Common Counsellors. I thought of dear Father, and saw many men whom I had seen when with him. Sir William Solesby spoke so highly of him to George. He said he was head and shoulders above the usual run of Common Counsellors and they had always so regretted that he had missed that one year in office. If he had not missed that, he would have been First Commoner.

The Maha Rajah spoke in perfect English, and was greeted with great enthusiasm. He spoke of the loyalty of India, a thrilling subject, and then General Smuts had a great ovation and made a fine speech, saying, among other things, that the Boers' reason for fighting was not loyalty to the Empire, but for the cause of righteousness and freedom, which is our cause. This will probably be the last Guild Hall function I shall ever go to.

May 18th. We have not yet heard from Jack, of his arrival. Reg says there is no need to be too worried.

The news from Russia is not good. The Socialist and Workmen's League have sent a strong appeal to the armies. Soldiers, it seems, are fraternising with the German soldiers, who, they are warned, are many of them officers in disguise. If only the Russians had fought now, we might have seen the end of the war this year.

July 22nd. Since I last wrote in this book, my dear Father has passed away. At 11 o'clock at night on May 26th, he entered into fuller life. I, and we all, are sure that the depression and anxiety caused by the war were the origin of his illness. We were most fortunate, in spite of the great demand for nurses, in being able to keep on Mother's nurse, and in getting an excellent male attendant as well. As I am writing incidents connected with the war, I will not write here about those last sad weeks. We had no difficulty about workmen to do the necessary work, nor horses for the carriages.

On Friday evening, July 20th, I received the following letter from Reginald about dear little Cecil.

During the last few days, we have been brought to realise the bitterness of war more than ever before. Last Friday, a cable from home brought the news of our dear brother, Cecil's, death; at the battle of Messines on the 7th June, our brave little laddie paid the supreme sacrifice after seven months of service in the field.

Though we saw so little of him, Jack said goodbye more than two years ago, we cannot help feeling it very deeply that we shall never see him again. You saw only a little of Cecil; he was a great lad, wholly unselfish, and good nature itself. We have cabled back 'we are proud of Cecil.' This last month must have been terrible for Mother, and although our divisions are only a few leagues apart, we have had no news till now. Jack has written to Cecil's C.O. and I have sent a note to a chap I know in the battalion, so we will let you know what we hear from them.

Thank you so much for your thought for us, and particularly for your goodness to Cecil. Now he will know your father, and we do not forget you went through such an experience as ours not long ago.

This letter shows the sort of boys those three are, and these are the boys who are laying down their lives for us in thousands and whom the Germans are killing. I pray that Jack and Reg may come through safely, and oh, that this terrible war might cease.

There has been a variety in the German attacks on London.

On Wednesday, June 13th, I had just got off the Moorgate St. bus in Blackheath Village when I heard aeroplanes, but these are so common round us that I did not even look up and thought that if the people lived in Highgate, they would not all be coming out of their shops, and staring. I did not even notice the guns, for one hears the Woolwich guns so plainly often, but just as I got onto the heath, I heard someone say 'Taubes', and then I looked up and saw 5 what looked like white butterflies high in the sky. I went into a shop, taking 2 little children in with me as everyone is told to take cover, and we watched them fly deliberately across the sky, followed later by one flying lower, but not one of our machines were visible. They had been sighted over the Nore 40 minutes before they got to London, and yet none of our machines went up. It was said that at Hendon most of the machines had no petrol in them and at one of the aerodromes a number were disabled.

When the firing was over, about 15 minutes, I went onto Brathay, and met Ethel who had cycled down from the canteen to see if Mother and Joyce were all right. We rang up George and Bernard, but could not get on to them. However, they rang us up and they both had had very horrid experiences. George had been in a train by Aldersgate Street station, and all the people were turned out into a tunnel, and the noise was deafening. Bernard had had a building struck quite close to his office, and he and his staff had gone down into the basement. Quinton had a very bad experience. Mary, Douglas and Frank happened to be in the office at the time. Bombs fell on the houses each side and in front of him. One fell in a little courtyard round part of which his place is built, and the street behind was devastated, and he only had 1 or 2 panes of glass broken. His men were very frightened, and the shock has made Mary quite poorly – affected her heart.

We went to Amersham on July 3rd for our holiday, for fares are so high now, 50% on every fare, and George wanted to be near town. On the 7th we were cycling, when I heard some deep continued booming at a great distance. It lasted quite 5 minutes or longer. We were to meet Mary Q. and Kathleen at the station at 1.08. They were coming for the Sunday. When we got to the station we at once heard rumours of an air raid, and when the trains came in, heard from the guard and from passengers that there had been a dreadful one. M. and K. did not arrive. Quinton came by the 3.16 and George met him, but no M. and K. so they were very worried, and we all went back to the station, and they appeared at 4.00. They had been hours getting to Liverpool Street from Woodford. We heard that the GPO was in flames, St Paul's hit and the Bank. None of this was true, but a telegraph station by the GPO was burned, and much damage was done to property but fewer people killed than in the last one. Everyone had been so strongly warned and urged to take cover. Also as it was Saturday, there were no children in the schools. One of the saddest things about the previous raid had been the many little children who had been killed. Bombs fell on several schools. Mrs Herbert Newton, who was staying with us, went to see a school mistress in one of these schools. She had saved the lives of all her children by moving them out of a certain larger room to another part of the building. She did this because there was a long passage from this room which she feared might be a death trap. The first room was literally wiped out by a bomb! The inspector, calling next day, pitched into this school mistress because she <u>had</u> moved the children! Though they would all have been killed if she had not. Red tape!

We have heard many accounts of the last raid. The aeroplanes came up in perfect formation, bomb droppers in the centre, battle planes around. They came slowly at a great height. When they passed over here there were about 40 of them. 22 Germans, the rest ours. Dr Bonsfield watched them all the time out of a top window with his glasses, and could see the fights going on distinctly, and the bombs dropping over the city, and the anti-aircraft guns firing. It must have been a wonderful sight. Several houses within a stone's throw of us were hit by shrapnel. Flo said the noise was deafening. She took the children into the cellar, and when she came out again, fully expected to see all the houses round in ruins. She did not realise that the city had been the objective, and thought it was Highgate that had been bombed and telephoned to that effect to Harold. Ethel's little Joyce counted 34 aeroplanes, and they saw at Blackheath our aeroplanes coming up all round the horizon. But ours were attacking in ones and twos, with no plan, and 4 of our men were brought down. It is dreadful. Ronald tells Quinton that his own flying squadron – one of the best – has come from the Front to guard London for a month until our own battle planes are ready. But one does not want the Front denuded of necessary machines for our safety. Ronald has been 'shocked' so badly that they say he will not be well for months. He has now gone to a hospital in the Isle of Wight. Many people were dreadfully unnerved by the last raid – Maud more than anyone I know. She can talk of nothing else and seems almost off her head. I am dreadfully sorry for both her and Harold. They are going to Brathay while Mother is here, as she feels safer in a larger house.

Last Sunday morning at 8.30 I heard a gun in the distance. I listened. Then another. I flew up. George likewise hurried on a dressing gown and went downstairs to the basement where we all stood with loud reports echoing all round. Then they got more distant and we said, 'They have been driven off.' It turned out to be only a warning. The first experiment of the kind! There had been a raid at Felixstowe and Harwich. At 10.20 a policeman cycled along calling 'all clear'. One had previously been seen with his warning placard on his breast. The warning frightened a lot of people more than the raid had done. For the future, we are to have 2 guns or rockets, instead of 3, and from fewer stations, but perhaps there will be no more.

July 26th. The papers lately have been full of bad news and today we read of the mutiny and retirement of the Russians in Galicia, and the annihilation of patriotic regiments, a cruiser and submarine sunk. The price of bread is to be lowered, consequently silly people like Mrs Norman Sargant and Street are going about saying there is plenty of food in the country, and there is no need to be so careful now, while Lord Rhondda says over and over again that unless the nation keeps on the same economical lines, our position will be more critical than it has been, and that he is reckoning on the continued self-denial of the nation.

July 28th. Dear Mother arrived yesterday to stay for 5 or 6 weeks. We have made the south room into a sitting room for her so that she need not come downstairs at all if she would rather not. She had to have a doctor's certificate before she could get a motor car. People can now get white bread – or rather flour for it, I think, if they have a doctor's certificate. Dr Bonsfield gave Mrs Carr one, with the 3 diseases she is suffering from entered very fully upon it. She refused to let her baker see it, but Dr B. could not get any flour or bread for her without it, so now it has gone up to Lord Rhondda! Miss Woodfirm, her sister, also wanted a certificate, but Dr B. said he could not possibly give her one. She says that war bread gives her indigestion, but Dr B. says he has 40 people worse than she is! She is very angry.

Lately the firing in Flanders has been terrific. They say the Somme battle was nothing to it. You can hear the guns distinctly, both here and at Blackheath, and there is something very solemn and terrible in the sound. It is a muffled, regular, far distant heavy boom – hardly a sound, more a feeling or impression.

Mr Dixon at Amersham told us some strange tales about the War Office. He was anxious to work for the country. He is a man of 48 or so and is a land surveyor. They told him they would need him the beginning of May so he hurriedly let his house to be all ready. At the end of the July he is still living at the Crown Inn waiting. They asked him if he understood machinery, and he said it was his hobby and he did understand a good deal in an amateur way of engines. They asked him if he could go into a Government workshop, look at the machinery made, and throw out what was not right. He said, 'Certainly not.' They said, 'I think you could,' and practically implored him to take the post. He absolutely declined (emolument £400 a year). A man he knows has got it, who does not know nearly as much about machinery as he did. He said to him, 'How had you the cheek to take it?' He said, 'Oh, I went into a workshop for a fortnight.'

Another man he knows was a soft goods advertising agent. He now goes about buying hay for the Government.

Our ships are still being sunk at just the same rate. We have not at all overcome the submarine menace, and Germany is pinning her hopes to it, although, as Mr Curtis pointed out to George, it is a great sign of weakness for Hindenberg, the militarist, to say that the hopes of Germany lie in the U-boat campaign.

August 6th. On Saturday, being the anniversary of our declaration of war, George and I went to a united prayer meeting of several churches in St Andrews parish hall, conducted by the vicar. George was asked to play. About 100 people I should think were there and it was a very nice little meeting. On Sunday we had the Russian national anthem in the morning and the American at night, and Grieg's 'O God protect our native land' as a solo. We have hardly a man left in the choir, and it is difficult to get any music. We had beautiful prayers, published by the SPCK, and a wonderful sermon in the morning from Mr Waights on 'the silences of God', to Herod, Pilate, Canaanish woman, and 'Be still and know that I am God' application to God's apparent silence in this war. After the evening service there was a great open air meeting in Pond Square, Highgate, Anglicans and non-conformists combined. The Vicar of Highgate told his congregation that the co-operation of non-conformists had been sanctioned by the Bishop! According to him, it was all right for them to meet in the open air! George went and said it was a fine service.

Sir Douglas Haigh began a great offensive on July 29th or 30th. The weather had been very dry and hot for a month, and on the 31st the weather broke, and we had phenomenal rain for the time of year for 4 days. This has terribly hampered our advance on the low lying Belgian coast and has allowed the Germans time to make good their defences and bring up their reinforcements. It is strange how often 'luck' goes against us. We cannot have learnt our lesson yet, but the nation stands firm for the same ideals that we had 3 years ago, and right the day must win – to doubt would be disloyalty – to falter would be sin.

August 18th. The weather the last 3 weeks has been very unsettled, and until a week ago the mud in Flanders was so dreadful that it was impossible to advance. The last week, however, there have been 2 great and successful pushes – one in the neighbourhood of Ypres, the other in the neighbourhood of Lens, but last night again there were deluges of rain. We have had a Sergeant Wagg from Masterton, New Zealand, staying with us for 2 nights. He came for a night last week and went to Scotland the next day, and on his return he came about 3.00 in the afternoon, and the next day we took him to Hampton Court, parting with him at Waterloo, at 6 o'clock, and by 6 o'clock the next morning he would be on his way to France. He was a very nice young fellow of 27. He had not slept in a home for 7 years, for he had parted with his father on unfriendly terms, and had been an engineer on ships, and then joined up when war began. He longs now to get home again, and he and his father are friends. He says the war has made him look at things in a very different light. He did not seem at all well. None of these boys do who come home on furlough, and one's heart aches for them. He is head of a 'shop' for mending guns, cycles, pistols, engines of all sorts, makes wrong fitments right etc. and his chief interest in Glasgow had been to go round munition places getting fresh ideas. He is a very intelligent boy and told us many interesting things. He said that the Belgian army is <u>rotten</u>, disloyal and full of spies. It has been taken completely from the front lines, and is only used for labour at the back. 2 first class French armies have taken its place on the Belgian coast, and we are seeing the consequence in this big push. They kept their trenches in a shocking state and he was one of our men sent to superintend others and help the French clean them up, and he himself saw German officers playing cards with Belgian officers in the trenches.

He also confirmed what all the soldiers say that the Belgians treat them abominably, even spoiling the wells, pumps etc. while the French will do anything for them.

He told us that the Germans have now a much faster flying machine than we have. Only one man is in it, and it is very tiny. He also said that after the London raid they were practically at the mercy of the German aeroplanes, so many had come over here from the Front. That was what I was afraid would happen, and I think we made too much of an outcry about the London raids. Why should we expect our soldiers to sit and be bombed, and an advance be stopped in order to ensure our safety. He told us how the Germans make observations. They fly low, and when they spot a gun or special object to fire at they turn sharp at right angles and immediately plop comes a shot. We do the same. All along the Front, at the distance of half a mile from each other, are observation balloons, and the same along the German line. Aeroplanes attack these balloons, and when they are seen approaching the men drop out with parachutes. Now only one man sits in the balloon, and it is generally possible for him to get safely to the ground. It was not possible for 2 to do so. Our men often drop incendiary bombs on them, and then there is no escape, and when a battle is beginning the first thing done is to demolish the observation balloons. He said that the taking of photographs when flying was very difficult and risky work. The camera is like a pistol and hangs over the side of the aeroplane. The observer has to look through and focus according to the height at which they are flying. Then when focused the aeroplane has to fly quite straight and this is the dangerous time. The observer also makes a drawing (I understood on the glass) at the same time. By this means they even get the trenches, and the lie of the trenches is also ascertained by raids. Then when thorough knowledge is gained by these means, an exact life-size model is built, and the great battles are rehearsed in full detail, even the barrage being represented by horses. Mr Wagg said it took months to rehearse for the present battle.

He says that often time hangs very heavy on their hands. They have nothing to do but play bridge, and large sums of money are lost and won. He must be a nice fellow, for his sister having died, and her husband having been killed, he wrote home to say he would be responsible for the 2 little children, and thought he could scrape up enough money to keep them at his father's. However, the boat was submarined and his letter lost, so they were sent to the husband's people in Sydney.

His conviction is that Ian Hamilton was not to blame for the fiasco of Gallipoli. He used to come to speak to them and say, 'They <u>will</u> not send me reinforcements,' and he says <u>many</u> times they could have got through if they had had more men, and more ammunition. They used to have 2 rounds a day for the big guns!

He had a very interesting time in Egypt. The men used to dig for curios, and 2 mummies were dug up by some soldiers, and they tried to smuggle them away, but were discovered and sentenced to 2 years' imprisonment. He found a gold ring which he sold for £50, and then the money was stolen from him! He told us how the Indian trick of the mango tree is done. When the plant is about 6 inches high, it is possible with care to pack it all back again into its seed, and then when the seed is watered it all bursts out again. An Arab had shown him this. The trick of making the big tree grow he believes is done by mesmerism. He has only come in at the end of this performance and has never seen anything, but other men have declared that they have seen it.

He had 10 days' leave, and does not expect to have another for a year. Will the war be over before then?

Yesterday, Lloyd George made a most encouraging speech in the House of Commons. He, at last, gave some details of the submarine results, and showed that July and August had been the best months for us since February, showing that our antisubmarine plans were taking effect. He also said that, with economy, there was plenty of food in the country for this winter. There is a wonderful increase in our output of merchant ships, and 330,000 tons have been bought. There has also been a large increase in the ships for the navy.

August 15th. On Wednesday, George said 5,000 American soldiers marched through London. He saw them in Trafalgar Square and there was great excitement and enthusiasm. They were a splendid set of men, and none had had more than 6 weeks' training. But George – and the papers – said they marched like veterans. Mr Wagg said they wore white spats and paper boots. He says there are already half a million in France, all equipped in the same way, and that they will all need fresh equipment.

It is almost unbelievable that America has already half a million men over, and this is a wonderful achievement. Some are already in the line and among the wounded. As Lloyd George said in his speech yesterday, 'if Russia had not failed us, the end would be in sight.' The Allies' plan had been to close in simultaneously. However, Russia is already pulling herself together now that the Germans are in her territory, but her failure this year has meant the prolonging of the war. Perhaps we are not yet ready for the end.

There is still excitement about the Stockholm Conference and we feel sorry that Mr Henderson is a Wesleyan. Perhaps the future may show his actions in a different light. The Pope also made his 'peace proposals' this week, but they have not found favour anywhere as they are distinctly pro-German. The Pope evidently does not understand the views or ideals of the Allies, shut up within 4 walls as he is. He speaks of 'useless slaughter'. We believe that through this terrible slaughter the highest ideals of man may be realised.

Our potatoes are a great success. All our vegetables have been, so it has been worth the while digging up so much of our garden.

September 6th. Mother is still staying with us, and we were so thankful that there had been no air raid, as since she was carried upstairs by Mrs Carr's gardener and nurse in Mrs Carr's chair, she has not been down, but has used the green room, made into a sitting room for her. On Tuesday, September 4th, I was reading in bed at 11.30 when I thought I heard distant guns, and in a minute Dorothy was knocking at the door. I woke George and ran into Mother's room, helped her to put on her jacket, warm petticoat and stockings, then ran into my own room to do the same and then Nurse, George and I got Mother down into the hall. She managed splendidly. We all sat in the hall, listening to the firing and the loud whirr of the engines, but could see nothing. The moon was brilliant, and the night still and clear, except for a ground mist. Alice got us hot milk and we gave Mother brandy. About 12.15 George objected to stopping up any longer, having upset the hot milk, and having nothing to do, so he went to bed. The search lights had stopped playing, and there was no sound of anything, so at 12.30 Mother wanted to go to bed, and we thought all was over. With great difficulty she toiled up, and 3 stairs from the top the guns and bombs began again. She could not turn on the stairs, and by the time she began to come down the noise was dreadful. One crash very near, and what's thought was the peppering of shrapnel over the house. She was wonderfully calm and brave. About 1.30 all was quiet again, and we made her and nurse beds up in the dining room, and we all went to bed.

Yesterday we found that a bomb had been dropped in the garden of Mrs Spencer, in between us and the station, about 6 houses away, another at Mrs Scarborough's in Crescent Road, another in St John's Road, Palace Road, and several other places in the neighbourhood. I went to see Mrs Spencer's today. It was a small bomb that had dropped there. It made a great hole in the lawn about 3 or 4 feet deep, and 5 or 6 wide. Every window that side of the house was smashed, and some of the window frames. The shutters were shattered, and a piece of the bomb had gone through plate glass, shutter, curtain on wall opposite, through the partition wall, a picture frame, and into the outer wall the other side of the house. It was a miracle no one was killed. I took a photo which I am afraid may come out badly as the light was bad.

A lady was killed with glass at Blackheath, but very few lives were lost, and very little damage done on the whole.

Last night we had one of the worst thunderstorms I ever remember, lasting from about 9.00 to 12.00, but one was so glad to feel that aeroplanes could not come in such weather, and that the flashes and bangs had not the Huns behind them.

Aunt Jennie came to see Mother today. It is the first time she has left Uncle John since his accident 7 weeks ago, and she was very nervous. I met her at the station with a cab, and dear old George took her all the way home again.

Mr Britton Jackson and his bride came to stay the night with us last week. He is a New Zealander, and being in hospital in Birmingham for some time with a bad wound, fell in love with his nurse. We did not think her equal to him and I rather think she is an RC. We had to put them in the top room as we had no other place to put them in, but they seemed very pleased to come and George gave them a cheque for £2.2.0 to buy a present with. They went on to Scotland the next day, and Lieutenant Jackson is going to New Zealand on September 30th to fetch home troops. His wife stays behind, as, if she went out with him, she would not be able to return. He left some of his luggage here. We have an accumulation of other people's belongings now.

September 9th. Sergeant Wright was to sail for Canada last Monday on a 2-month furlough and then he hopes to take a commission and to go to America to train troops. He would not be of any use in the army for some time as he has trench feet.

He came to say goodbye in great spirits, and brought his photograph for us, and could not say enough about what we had done for him. We shall quite miss him and his 'fine'. He is 6 ft 4. He is only 21 and must have a good deal of character. He was a sergeant to serve out rum to the men when a charge was made, and he never took any himself. The last time but one that he came here he said he should try to come oftener as it must be 'lonesome' for us alone! He sent to Canada for some maple sugar for me, and says he will send us a Canadian Methodist hymn book. I wonder if he will remember.

Mr Myers and family sailed for Adelaide last Monday week. It is almost impossible to get passports for women and children now, so I suppose he got his on account of John's health. We gave him deckchairs, and had the greatest difficulty in getting them as none are made now. However, George got them wholesale. I trust he and his family will arrive safely. They were being convoyed. They had been waiting to go for months. Mr and Mrs Trevor Davies have been waiting to get off to Canada for quite 2 months. The submarine menace is just as serious, and our losses just about the same, though Lloyd George speaks most hopefully. The great offensive has fizzled out again. We thought it would be continued when the weather improved (August was the wettest on record for very many years) but though it has been comparatively fine, things have been quiet. The wretched Huns are now deliberately bombing the <u>hospitals</u> behind the lines. The

Russians are retreating rapidly from Riga, and the news from there [from the Russian frontier] gets worse and worse, but it is said that the Germans cannot get to Petrograd this year as it is too late in the season. A lot of damage has been done to the harvest by the weather, and the papers are rather dismal reading. When they are too depressing, I only read the summary of news, as it does no one any good to be depressed. In fact, cheerfulness is obligatory just now. Our own potato crop is excellent.

Maud has been awfully upset by the aeroplane raids. She was at first most anxious that Harold should get transferred somewhere, and she hates her house and hates Blackheath. One is dreadfully sorry for both her and Harold. They have been staying at Brathay all the while Mother has been away and for some time before she came here. Maud feels safer there, and I expect they will be with Mother a good deal this winter.

Ethel and the children have been to Holmwood in Surrey for the holiday and the children, especially Honor, have been helping 'on the land', milking cows etc. Submarines bombed Scarborough last week, but it was nothing like the first bombardment.

Milk is going to be 8*d* a quart.

This afternoon [Sunday] we had another scare of a raid and we brought Mother down. The specials were out, and people sent home. You see them running through the streets. But the raiders did not get to within 30 miles of London. The SS children went home.

September 29th. Our Harvest Festival tomorrow and we have been decorating the church this afternoon. Eggs have been asked for instead of fruit and flowers, as the hospitals need so many, so we had not much to work with, except what Mrs Norman and we sent.

At about 6.15, Tom Sargant, who had been up to fetch their own eggs and very kindly brought mine down too, came in with the news that the air raid warning was out – a green light on the tram centres. All of us vanished like smoke, as a Special said there was time to get home. Mrs Norman and I came up together, and we called on Mrs Ream to tell her. She asked me to go in there till George got home, but I thought I had better come home. George promised to be in by 7.

It is nearly 7 now and there is no sound of guns, so the raid may have been turned back. It was last night, and some machines brought down. We heard distant guns about 9 o'clock.

On Monday, October 1st, the Taubes and Gothas came about 8.15 and the noise was terrific. A new mode of fighting them had been adopted – a barrage of fire – and it proved most successful. Only 2 got through, and these dropped bombs on the Bedford Hotel, Southampton Row, where 6 people were killed, and one in Dean's Yard, Westminster, and another near the Palace. The noise was great, and once I thought an aeroplane must have come down on the house, and the men have got out, and pounding about. I and Elizabeth and Alice sat in the dining room. George was at the school and the people came crowding in there, but the Wesley Guild was having its 'social' and they went on with music and games.

On Tuesday, there was another raid, but no machines got through to London, though the firing went on, as before, for about 1½ hours. The tubes have been crowded with people, mostly aliens, who have gone in about 5 o'clock and encamped for the night, taking cushions etc. with them. It became impossible for travellers to get in or out of trains, and there was danger of people getting pushed onto the line, and also of serious infection. I went to Belsize Park by tube yesterday and the smell of disinfectants was enough to knock you down. So now the people are not allowed in unless a raid is imminent. On Wednesday there was no raid, due, the papers said, to the fact that our airmen had bombed 15 Gothas lying ready to start. Poor little Phoebe had been so upset with the raids of Monday and Tuesday evenings that she had 2 bad fits on Wednesday morning. They were all going to Amersham that day to avoid raids! The poor mite had ice bags on her head all Wednesday, and on Thursday they decided to take her down in a motor, Dr Parry going with them, as they considered this a lesser risk than chancing another raid. She is none the worse for the journey. She had a soothing draught, and slept most of the day.

George and I had a week at Amersham after Mother left us, and saw the cousins at Wendover. They are probably staying away till after the Hunter's moon.

Since last writing, our troops have made another successful advance in the neighbourhood of Ypres, and the weather lately has been beautiful. Another Australian came up with George on Thursday, September 27th – a Mr Coleman from Sydney, a man with 7 children. It is <u>fine</u> of him to come.

Fred Savage has been killed. First Howard, then Fred. I pray that the 2 other boys may be preserved.

October 5th. Bertram has got his discharge from the army, and expects to be home next Saturday. Poor Mary Q.'s nerves have been so upset by that raid she was in that she and Kathleen have gone away for 3 months.

Mr Maude, who has just been staying with us, came home from West Africa in a convoy. There were 7 ships, some of them big Castle liners. They met at a certain port, and started out with an armed merchant man, and when they were about a day's sail from land they were picked up by 8 destroyers. The armed cruiser went first, followed by 2 ships then 3, then 2, and the destroyers went 4 on each side like wings. I wonder they don't convoy all the ships. Perhaps they do! Mr Maude says it is difficult now to get food in West Africa. They depend so much on tinned stuff, and all this now has to come from America. He wonders very much what they will do for food when he gets back. The brave old man is over 70.

My Dorothy is leaving after having been here 5 years, but her sister is getting 30/- a week in business, and she thinks if she gets the same she can put by more towards the time when her husband leaves the army (she went for 16/- a week). We have been most fortunate to keep our 3 when numbers of people have none. I advertised, and put into 2 registry offices, and asked everyone I knew, and only heard of 2 maids. One wanted 2 nights and half a day a week in order to learn typewriting to go into business in March! I have engaged a nice little maid from a home for servants. She is only 16, but looks very bright, and I am fortunate to have got her. But it will seem odd to have such a young thing again.

September 30th. George got in last night about 7.15 and at 8.45 we heard the guns begin, and we had a very bad time. We went into the kitchen, and the firing was continuous, shells whistling round us, and engines humming, and occasionally a loud deep dreadful noise like a bomb. We stayed down there till it got quiet about 10.15. The trains ran dark until 12.15, but we went to bed between 11.00 and 12.00. This morning we heard that a bomb or shell had dropped on the front of the chapel and on the steps, but not doing much damage. 2 or 3 bombs had dropped near Hornsey Road chapel, and every window is smashed, and the roof riddled with shots, but a public house at the corner of Hornsey and Seven Sisters roads had its basement blown away, leaving the upper storeys standing, supported on iron pillars. Many were killed here.

Some of our choir left London today. We managed an anthem this morning, but poor Mrs Hancock who took the solo was so shaky that she nearly broke down. This evening we had the service at 5.30 and we had a wonderful congregation considering that it was only known this morning. Much better than an ordinary morning congregation. There were only 8 girls in the choir and 5 men so we could not have an anthem. On our way home, we went into Dr Bonsfield's to see how they had got on, and while we were there the guns began. We hurried home, and had a repetition of last night for about 1¼ hours. It is very terrible, and I do wish the weather would change. Today is full moon, and the evenings are cloudless and absolutely still.

Saturday, October 13th. On Monday, September 30th, we had another air raid, and it lasted 3 hours, but we had no bombs so near us as on the Saturday and Sunday nights. On Sunday night a bomb fell in the grounds of St Aloysius school, just the other side of the Archway, but in the earth, and another dropped on the porter's lodge on Dartmouth Park Hill, just by Waterloo Park. People left London in droves. In May's road there are only themselves and one other family left. We stayed on because it does not seem fair to go when so many – the poor, doctors, clergymen, businessmen – cannot go, and it might very much incense the East End if all the people with money get themselves into safety. The raids do not injure our health at present, and we have no children to think for, and we have duties at home which it does not seem right to run away from. Many others of course feel the same.

There has been no raid since September 30th, but I had a great fright on October 1st. I had been to the dentists, and at Finsbury Park a lady in the train told me that the streets were being cleared as a raid was imminent. Just as I got outside Crouch End station, the first bang went, and then they followed thick and fast. Everyone ran, and the lane was cleared in the twinkling of an eye. I thought I would run home, as our home was so near, but I could not run up the hill! I debated whether I would go into one of the houses, but decided I would try to get home. I passed Dr Bonsfield in his car at the gate. Just as Alice opened the door to me there was a loud report apparently just overhead, and we rushed into the kitchen where the maids and Sister Nellie were sitting in the dark with the shutters fastened. In a minute or two all was quiet again, and <u>then</u>, and not till then, it struck me that these were the warning maroons, and no raid! Which turned out to be the case, but everyone else was taken in too. I went in the afternoon to the Red Cross sewing meeting, and hardly anyone was there.

People had got very nervy. One can't help feeling very anxious about this next moon, but after then the danger will probably be over for the present. I wish Mother could be out of it, but she will not leave all of us, and indeed we think that the dangers of cold, and not being able to have her own doctor if she went away, are more serious than of staying where she is – at any rate till the spring. I do not know what Harold will do. Maud is very nervous and keen on him getting a transfer. It is very doubtful if he could, even if he tried, and he is not worried. He wants Maud to go away. She stayed at Bournemouth till after the last raid.

In the 8 days we had 6 raids, but only 26 people were killed, which shows the advantage of taking cover.

October 12th. Mr Arnold came up to see us yesterday. It is 16 months since he was last home, and he feels it very much that his battalion, which is not supposed to be under fire, is working only 5 miles from the Front, and they are continually under fire. They have sometimes, too, been very short of food. He says there are thousands of Chinese labourers now – very smart and good workers – who will do anything for their captains. He blew the organ on Sunday and said his Amens so loudly and did enjoy himself, poor man.

There is every prospect of food being very short this winter. Last week in Crouch End we could not get butter, bacon, tea nor matches. Bacon, when you <u>can</u> get it, is

2/6 a lb, butter 3/-. We were getting short of matches and George went to a number of tobacconists in town, and succeeded in getting 6 boxes, and on Saturday Dorothy arrived with 2 dozen boxes which her sister had managed to get from her shop. Pork cannot be got because the farmers can make no profit in selling at the price the government allows, and it is cheaper for the farmers to sell milk than butter. Therefore they don't trouble to make butter. Milk next month is to be 8*d* a quart. Meat is 1/8 to 1/10. Steak much more. Sausages 1/9 a lb.

October 23rd. Last Thursday we went to a lecture in Christ Church lecture hall given by an officer, a Captain Nobbs, who had been blinded at Mons and kept a prisoner in Germany for a long time. He told us some most interesting things. There were 8 officers – 4 French and 4 English – in the hospital, and about 50 Tommies, and it was a hospital for venereal disease and the soldiers used to be operated upon in the morning, the Germans in the afternoon, and the men of honour and the men of dishonour take their exercise together in the garden.

The doctor was a fine fellow, but there was no nursing. There was a French orderly in the room with the officers and Captain Nobbs said what they owed to the unselfish devotion of that man no words could tell. A Russian soldier did the bandaging. The food the officers had would have been fair for a man in health, but almost impossible for sick men to eat, but the poor Russians would stand for hours in crowds on the chance of 2 of them being told off to carry in the officers' dinner and getting a little soup given them. Captain N. said he quite enjoyed that soup, but the others said he would not have if he could have seen it.

After he was discharged from hospital he and the doctor hoped he would have been sent home, but for some reason he was kept in Germany and sent from camp to camp. He said, poor man, that he kept his 'eyes' open and connected it to his 'ears' to learn all he could about the treatment of the prisoners, and it is through him that their condition has been partially ameliorated, and that many have been moved to neutral countries. Officers, not men, for the men are made to work and so are of value to Germany. It is against the law of nations for officers or non coms to be made to work, but the Germans got over that difficulty by putting their non coms all together in one camp and then drilling them for 10 hours a day with only 1 minute's rest the end of each hour. This, combined with the poor food, compelled these men to volunteer to do work. For breakfast, the soldiers' food was a cup of acorn coffee and 2 slices of bread, one of which they had to save for supper, soup like water, with occasionally a potato in it for dinner, and acorn coffee again for supper. They would literally starve if it were not for the parcels sent from home. These generally reach them safely. There seems to be no systematic robbing of these.

He told us of 80 men in one of the camps who were marched off to work. When they got to the place they found it was munition work, and refused to do it. They were told they would be shot if they did not do it. They still refused. They were then lined up against a wall, they still refused, the order to fire was given but the cartridges were blank and the men were marched back to the camp and imprisoned for 14 days.

Other men were ordered to do similar work, they likewise refused. One by one they were asked if they still refused and one by one taken out and those left heard the shot fired, but all remained firm and when the last man went out he found all the others there! At another camp, on refusal to do this sort of work, men were imprisoned separately for 4 days and at the end of that time when the doors were opened they were nearly starved. The German commandant said he should not punish them any more as he did not know Englishmen had so much grit.

The men liked working on the farms best, for though the hours were tremendous, from 5.00 a.m. to 10.00 p.m., the farmer would be kind to them sometimes and the food was often better. Prisoners are not treated quite so badly now; for one thing we have 3 times as many prisoners as they have and their ideas of the Englishmen have somewhat altered. Also, now the Germans are civilian soldiers like ours, and not quite the cruel brutes they used to be.

When the American inspectors came round the camp, in some cases the commandants would allow them to mix freely with the prisoners and talk to them privately, but in one camp it was put up that if anyone made a complaint they would have 14 days' imprisonment. The Americans came round between the commandant and another officer who never left them. 2 men dared to complain and got their 14 days.

One did admire the pluck of this poor blind captain. He was a big fine looking man, but he had not a very strong voice and George could not hear one sentence, though we sat in the very front.

October 28th. On October 8th, Jack Dunn had his foot blown off. The Germans were shelling the wounded 'whether by accident or not', Reg said. 'He was very brave. He sat up and held the artery telling the men to look after the others, but the others were all dead, and we think this very episode is the one described in *The Times*.' Reg was with him that day and the next and saw him off into a hospital train, and he wrote to me 2 days after getting to Étaples, the base hospital in France. Then we heard no more until October 26th when a letter came from Birmingham, and I had gone up on the 25th to Birmingham to speak at a meeting and then I got home and found his letter. It was maddening, but George is going to try to see him on Tuesday when he goes to Oxford. One does feel most awfully for the boy, and for poor Reg left alone in France. And one feels now as if this war may drag on for years. Russia collapsing in this way is a terrible blow to the Allies, and yesterday in the paper we read of Germany's blow against Italy – 30,000 prisoners, according to the German account. The Germans had been brought from the Russian front, and wherever the Germans go, they succeed, except upon the West Front. They are no match there for our men and the French, though if they can bring their armies from the Russian Front, one wonders what sheer weight of numbers may do. It is terrible to think of our men having another winter in France and Flanders. They are fighting now in water to their waists and even shoulders. They are the most glorious heroes, and so gay, and the men who have not yet gone are so keen on getting out.

We had a young soldier, Roderick Piper – another Adelaide boy – who had been at school with Cecil Dunn, to spend the evening last Friday. He could not stay as he was to spend the Sunday at the Agent General's. He is only 19, a fine looking boy, and so keen on getting to Flanders. He is in the Australian 32nd, known as the fighting 32nd. Whenever they go to the Front, they know hard fighting is to follow. He told us some of their casualties. On July 1st 1916 (when Howard was killed) they went in 1,200 strong, and came out <u>150</u>. They have been in 4 great attacks, and have come back between 100 and 200 each time. This boy has chosen this regiment and he is a machine gunner in it. It is wonderful. It makes one long to do something. I feel sometimes as if I long to be a man, and to fight, and then I wonder if I might not have been a coward. It must be a great help to be trained and know exactly one's duty. I am always afraid that in an emergency I may be found wanting.

We asked Miss Bedells in for the evening as Roderick said he would much rather stay here than go to a theatre. The boys seem to like some home life and a girl, if possible!

October 17th. Bertram Thomas spent a night last week with us. He has total exemption from the army and is back at home, but he would far rather have been fit to return to France! He was in the trenches for 2½ months. The plan in France is 8 days in the trenches, 8 resting. Of the 8 days in the trenches, 2 are in the front line, 2 in the second and 4 in reserve. It is difficult to get to the trenches. It has to be done in the dark – a march of several miles, and the last 2 miles over a narrow plank from which if you slip you fall into mud perhaps 3 feet deep. You shave in water from the puddles. I asked Bertram how he was sent back and it was a most providential sort of story. The colonel or captain came along to arrange about the men going over the top and he said to Bertram, 'How do you feel about it?' and he replied that of course he was quite ready to do whatever was required. He said he knew that, but was he 'fit' and he told him that he could march all right, but could only run about two-thirds as fast, but in the excitement he should probably do as well as they did. However, the captain said he had another job he should send him to. The sergeant was sorry as he had also some lighter thing for him to do. However, that night he and a few others were marched off some miles to another regiment. When they got there, no one was expecting them, and they had to bivouac right under some guns. The bivouac is to lie on the ground covered with canvas. Bertram said it was a most dangerous position and none of them cared about it.

About 11.00 p.m. some man in authority came along, and asked whatever they were doing there, and they must not stay there and ordered them back to their regiment. When they got back, they were not wanted there (something had fallen through about the sergeant's work) and Bertram, who had bad sciatica, was ordered in to rest camp with the others. There his temperature was taken, and was high! He was most surprised – he was ordered into hospital – sent to the base, then to Nottingham, and finally was given total exemption.

He looks very well and his sciatica does not trouble him much. It is providential I think.

We are in the very middle of the Hunter's moon. The weather has been lovely the last few days, and the moon brilliant every night. Today [Sunday] we had service at 5.30 but we have as yet had no alarms, and now we are hoping that we shall not, and that the aeroplanes find it too cold. Our anti-aircraft guns fire about 1,500 ft high, and this makes it necessary for the aeroplanes to fly so high to keep out of range that their engines get frozen. This is the theory now, for there really seems to be no other reason why the Germans should not attempt a raid. All the people who have gone away for this moon will feel sorry they went.

We had a most curious experience on Friday evening [19 October]. Mr Dixon from the Home Office was with us, and we all went down to a missionary committee at the church. While there, at 8.20 the warning was given. We could not make out for it was a dark night (very dark, for when we were standing waiting for the bus, a man walked right into me, and nearly knocked me down). Most of the people promptly departed.

Norman Sargant came in just as the warning was given, said he must get home to his wife and went straight back. We stayed on, at about 9 o'clock started home. The people were crowding into the schoolroom and two guns (which turned out afterwards to have been bombs) were heard.

George and I started home. Mr Dixon followed about 10 minutes later, and I was very thankful when we got home. I didn't think we met more than two people, but there was no sound of guns. Mr Dixon rang up the Home Office and heard that it was a very widespread Zeppelin raid. They got to Birmingham, Bedford, Wendover and I don't know where. We thought we should certainly hear guns if they came to London, so we went to bed soon after 11, and about 11.30 I heard a noise and the windows shook, but nothing further occurred. It was something – an explosion perhaps – very far away.

But the next morning we found that it had been a very serious Zeppelin raid. The bomb at 11.30 was probably the one in Piccadilly, just off the Circus. Every window the Piccadilly side of Swan & Edgars was smashed, and all the windows of the restaurants, Cabin, Slaters, Lyons, ABC etc. opposite. Also the great bank windows. The bomb fell on the road, making a hole about 6 feet deep and killing several pedestrians. Although the 'all clear' signal had not been given, as time went on people hearing no guns thought all was right. We have never yet had a Zeppelin over London without firing going on, and we have not been told why there was none. Bombs were dropped at Hither Green, Lewis Lane, Hampstead and about 30 people killed. However, something happened to the Zeppelins whether by the tactics of our men or not, for they got lost and their machines would not act because of the cold, and they drifted over France and 4 were brought down by French airmen in the daylight, right in the South of France, and it is thought that another was lost in the Mediterranean.

About 2 o'clock that night we were woken by a bugle. I jumped up, put my dressing gown on and woke George, but nothing further happened so we went to bed again and it turned out to be a new 'all clear' signal!

October 29th. I stayed with Lady Barnsley in Birmingham. Her husband and 3 sons are at the war and a fourth has been killed. She has one daughter at home, and a sister-in-law, a Mrs Marriott, and her daughter living with her, as her husband is in France too.

Families are so mixed up now, and everything is so different. It is a very difficult time to start this great Women's Auxiliary Fund, but the openings abroad are so wonderful and God's work cannot stop. Our conference was quite a success, delegates coming from all parts of England.

November 19th. We heard afterwards that a Zeppelin had got through without being observed. It must have shut off its engines and drifted, so there was no sound, and there was a good deal of mist about.

Last week was the lowest in losses of ships by submarines that we have had since February. Only one large ship was sunk, but it is considered likely that this is only the lull before some new devilry begins. We have had no raids since the Zeppelin one, but the new moon is just beginning. However, we don't expect any more raids till the spring. Numbers of people have left London 'for the period of the war'. Mrs Waights has been away since July 16th, and several other people at Hornsey have followed her example, leaving their husbands behind. Several of our girls in the choir have taken situations in the country. Mrs Sitchfield and her daughters have gone. It much disorganises church work, and I think these people will feel rather foolish for deserting their duties if there should be no more raids this winter.

October 29th. Poor Italy have had their terrible disaster at Caporetto since I last wrote. They are now making a stand on the Plave, and British and French troops are being rushed to their help. There has been the meeting between Lloyd George and French and Italian prime ministers at Rapallo, and the decision to have a war committee of 3 – Sir Harry Wilson, General Cadorna and General Weygand – and it is hoped that America and Russia will join. The frankness of Lloyd George's Paris speech has been much criticised, and there is an acute political crisis, which culminates tomorrow, and one feels very anxious. Lloyd George has done wonders for the country. He is a strong man, though he may be a 'bounder', and no doubt he has many enemies who will try to shake the confidence of the country in him.

November 18th. George was at a political dinner last night, the first since the war began, and our member 'Kennedy Jones' seemed very much against him. He says it is taking the war out of the hands of the military and placing it in the hands of the politicians, and that if tomorrow shows that L. G. has not the military behind him, he will oppose him. But I cannot think that he would have taken such a step if he had not the military behind him. K. J. is of the Harmsworth family – therefore American. I only hope L. G. won't be so heckled that he resigns in a temper. We don't want political divisions now.

Mr and Mrs A. L. Dixon have been staying with us, and I think Elizabeth thinks we ought not to have visitors in war time, for she has the most extraordinary ideas, and expresses herself very unpleasantly sometimes. She is an old socialist. But in some ways she is very good. I think the difficulty of getting things puts her out, though really we have had to go without nothing yet, except once or twice to have margarine instead of butter, and that is not much hardship. Some people have had difficulty in getting tea and yesterday when I went to get cake for soldiers, they told me it was the last plum cake they would have, as it was impossible to get raisins or currants. Fortunately we made plum pudding last year and I kept 2 for this year, but I don't think we shall be able to make mincemeat. The new voluntary rations are out.

Meat		2 lbs a head a week
Bread	Men on sedentary work	4 lbs 8 oz
	Women on sedentary work	3 lbs 8 oz
Domestic service		4 lbs 0 oz
Butters, margarine, lard, oils and fats		10 oz
Cereals other than bread		12 oz

It will be very difficult with the fats, and rather difficult with the meat. 10 lbs a week, one quarter of which must be bone, and to include suet is very short allowance for 5 people, including breakfast meat. For sweetening puddings now we use golden syrup.

Harold is ill at Brathay, from overwork and worry, and we are very anxious about him. Maud had agitated until she got him to exchange from Woolwich to Warwick, and they were both to have gone after Christmas but it is doubtful if Harold will be able to. Mother would feel parting with him dreadfully, but if it is for the dear boy's good we shall all be content. I do not know what arrangements can be made about Mother. We should not like her to be alone. The work of paymasters is very heavy and the hours long. Harold sometimes has to be off at a quarter to 8 and would not be home till 7. Remuneration £200 a year. Possibly Warwick may be a quieter office with more regular work and hours. The doctor says it is hard work and worry that has brought this on. The war makes life difficult in many ways. It is such a period of unrest. People leave their homes and let them, and the hotels are full – maids are unsettled, munition and other workers getting such high wages. There are no end of marriages, before the men go out, or when they are home on leave. Rationing is difficult and the strain and sadness of the war make people's tempers uncertain. It is difficult to get work done, and incompetent people are doing things.

March 20th. Lloyd George came off with flying colours. Of course, he had the military behind him all the time, and this plan had actually been proposed by Kitchener 2 years ago. Today we heard of the death of Sir Stanley Maude, the hero of Baghdad and the Mesopotamian campaign – a most brilliant general. The Germans are nearer Venice, though the Italians are now fighting bravely. Sometimes it seems as if everything is against us, and one wonders. We have many sins to reproach ourselves with: drunkenness, opium, the white slave traffic, but surely the Germans have many more.

Yesterday I saw 2 girls driving a high 'Royal Mail' cart. The girl guards on the trains wear very smart uniform coats about to their knees, and gaiters. The girls on the land look as if they have just stepped off the stage – wide felt hats turned up at the side, light farm coats not to their knees and brown gaiters. It is a most becoming costume. The women porters at some of the stations wear short fawn-coloured overalls or coats, and sort of mob caps drawn over their heads, and the women who clean the carriages wear butcher's blue or heliotrope. The window cleaners in town often wear similar uniforms, white with white trousers. At George's dinner the other night all the waiters were either very old or young boys in white aprons.

January 14th, 1918. It is nearly 2 months since I wrote this journal. I have wanted to do so often, but have been so very busy and the time goes so quickly.

The Italian disaster was very grave, and French and British were rushed up to help the Italians, and now they are making a good stand, but our 3rd Army, which was a particularly fine one, was sent, which has considerably weakened our striking power in the West. It must be very disappointing for our commanders. Since the Ypres offensive in October and November we have been purely on the defensive. Lately the weather has been too bad for anything to be done, first through rain and mud, and now through frost and snow. The Australian casualties in October alone were 40,000 – nearly half the fighting strength. These particulars do not get into the papers.

Lloyd George came triumphantly out of the political crisis on November 20th, and he proved to have been in consultation with the military all the time, as one was sure he would be, but the Russian debacle goes from bad to worse. Lenin now is defying the bourgeoisie of England and France as well as Germany, and says that Russia will take up arms against them all. Trotsky has, according to today's papers, given in to the German demand that the peace discussions shall continue at Brest-Litovsk instead of at Stockholm as Russia demanded. In today's paper also one reads of the murder of Russian admirals by the Bolsheviks. Some of the papers regard the Bolsheviks as children with great ideals, which ideals they think they can oppose to German militarism, and these papers consider it a very fine and wonderful thing. But, even if this is so, Russia has been a traitor to the Allies, and it is owing to her that 10,000 of our splendid men have lost their lives.

Jack Dunn came up to Southall early in December 1917 and Millicent and I went over to see him. The hospital there is for men wanting limbs or eyes, and there are hundreds of them. I thought it a terrible sight. Jack met us at the door and we went out with him to tea. He is extraordinary on his crutches. After that, he often came here. He got from 1.30 to 10.00 every other day, so he used to get here about 4.00 and leave at 8.00. It seemed a very long, tiring journey for such a short time. Twice he went to Ethel's, and Mrs G. Corderon and Mrs Jack Matthews both asked him out at Ealing. Then he got furlough the Saturday before Christmas, and stays with us until January 22nd, when he will have to return to hospital for his leg and then will probably be sent almost at once back to Adelaide. A boat-load of disabled men went a day or two ago, and there is to be one more, and then probably not another one for 6 months, as the boats are to be used for bringing over the American army. These boats will probably take Australians back to America, but no further.

The boy looks a wreck and it makes one's heart ache to see him. We have fed him up as much as possible and given him a strong tonic, but I think he really needs fresh air and sunshine and a non-war atmosphere, which he will get to a certain extent in Australia, for everyone says it is impossible to really realise the war there. He gets along very quickly on his crutches, and hops about the house, never using them in the house. He hops upstairs, and swings down and is like an acrobat getting down from the tops of buses. On Christmas Day, on our way to Brathay we went to the service at St Paul's. It was a sunny cold morning and the cathedral looked beautiful with the sun pouring in. The music was beautiful too, but I did wish the great congregation had joined in the Christmas hymns. Then, as there was no train, we took the bus to Blackheath and at London Bridge, after waiting a long time, it came in packed. 3 people got off and we were at the back of the crowd. There was no chance of our getting on, but the conductress pushed the crowd back and called out, 'Tommy first,' and Jack said, 'No, I have 2 friends,' and she called, 'Tommy and his friends' and we got on! Much the same thing happened at Finsbury Park. Jack and I had got onto the usual platform, when we found the train went from another one. It was just starting, and I thought there was no chance of getting round, but the porter said, 'I'll keep it for you.' I told him we could not hurry, and when we got onto the platform we found the guard in such a fume wondering what he was kept waiting for, and with a first class carriage door open into which we walked as if we had first class tickets. It is very nice that everyone is so good to wounded men and so they ought to be.

We spent Christmas at Brathay. Jack at Ethel's and he had a very lively time there. George and I went in to tea and had music and the Toy Symphony and much noisy fun. Of course at Brathay it was very quiet. We had dear Father constantly in our minds and Harold is so poorly. We are very anxious about the darling. He has diabetic symptoms and sclerosis of the nerves, brought on by worry over work. Another piece of work of this dreadful war. It has all sorts of side issues. He is on a very strict diet, and goes to bed early, gets up about the middle of the morning, takes a short walk, lies down again in the afternoon and is fed up as much as his diet allows. Mother is so glad to have him with her to take care of.

January 11th, 1918. He and Maud come to us tomorrow for a long visit. They have let their own house, and have been living at Brathay for some time. Maud is less nervous of raids in the larger house. Harold saw a specialist – Farquhar Buszard – in December and is to see him again in March.

Dear Mother was wonderfully bright and brave at Christmas time. She is so anxious to appear all that a Christian should be to Miss Davies, who thinks that Christians should not grieve! I hope she is not putting too great a strain upon herself. Of course she is much more of an invalid than she was but she is getting through the winter wonderfully. She has no cold at present. Her bodily comforts are most carefully and well looked after by Miss Davies.

Jack fell down at Ethel's on his stump and when he came back to us I had Dr Bonsfield in and he had a very bad place and had more or less to lay up for quite a week, and it is not right yet. He caught his foot in a piece of carpet. Honor came for 2 or 3 days and we have had girls in, and made things as cheerful as possible for him, but I feel sad whenever I look at him or at Harold, and there is so much sorrow in the world now – though there is also much to be thankful for. But sometimes the sorrow seems overpowering and yet it is our duty to keep bright, because depression affects the morale of the nation. I have taken up my Wednesday class again, and have been visiting the women. Nearly all have husbands, brothers or sons at the war. Many have lost those they love, others are severely wounded or missing. Then these women now may spend hours in food queues, for meat, tea or margarine. They will wait for hours, and yet I heard no complaints and all spoke so bravely and resignedly. It made one proud of them.

1918. On Sunday, January 6th, we had the day of National Intercession and it was a wonderful day. We had good congregations, but one heard everywhere of crowded churches, and even queues. We had the church intercession service in the morning, and our own at night, both beautiful services, and in the morning we had a lovely quartet of Grieg's 'O God protect with Thy strong hand our children and our native land', sung by

Mrs Rockett, Hilda Greenwood, Norman Sargant and Jack. Everyone was delighted with Jack's voice. We had the S.P.G. prayer service in the morning and our own at night, with special hymns and an anthem at night, 'God shall wipe away all tears'. If only the nation would turn to God.

February 1st. Harold and Maud left us last Friday. We have had a very full time, for Jack got extension of furlough, and also a friend of his, Bert Chesters, turned up on leave from France of 14 days. He came to us from a Saturday till Monday night when he went up to Scotland, and came back to us on the following Monday, and stayed till Friday. Jack was with us part of the time but had to go back to hospital to get his leg fitted. He is finding it very difficult to manage and it chafes him a good deal. He exercises it for about 2 hours a day, but is the rest of the time on his crutches. He has every other day out from 1.30 to 10 o'clock. Last Thursday he left us at a quarter to 9 and did not get to Southall till 12.15, there was such a fog and this has happened more than once, but he thinks it worth coming. Miss Bedells often comes in to have music with him, and Ethel has had him over several times. Today we have had letters from Mr and Mrs Dunn who seem so grateful for what we have been able to do for their boys, but it is little enough.

This is a time of great unrest. Things got so uncomfortable in the kitchen that I had to give Elizabeth notice, but we understand each other better now. Then Alice was so overdone by so many visitors and Hester's incapacity that she gave notice to leave in May and I had already given Hester notice. Elizabeth has been here 18 years, Alice about 12, so I felt very miserable. I was most fortunate to hear of a young maid through Mother, and I much hope she may turn out as Dorothy did. I have also been fortunate in getting a very nice woman belonging to my class to come in a day a week to help Alice. We were most fortunate too in food while the house was so full of visitors. Harold and Florence and the Norman Sargants have not had a joint since Christmas and I know of nobody who has had a proper joint, and we have had joints each week varying from 8½ to 6 lbs, and a certain amount of chops and steaks during the week, so with the help of rabbits, fish and poultry we have managed, even with all our visitors, and Harold has had fresh meat every day. I have not been able to understand why we have been so specially favoured. They say that I smile at the butchers and the joints roll up! Our grocer lets us have all the fats he can. I had tea with Mrs Huntsman Barrett 2 or 3 weeks ago and though she deals with the same butcher grocer, she had had no fats for 10 days! And we had thick sandwiches of paste with no butter. We have never been without butter or margarine and while I had all these visitors Emma Creary got me one lb of butter and one of margarine. Mr Mellor from the office sent me a lb of butter, and dear old Mrs Maude managed to get me half a lb in Yelverton. I had got some bacon and ham while it was still gettable, so we did splendidly – but of course kept within our ration.

Bert Chesters is a very nice boy, aged 23, fair as a girl. His father is a tea merchant in Ipswich, Brisbane, Queensland, and he has been through Gallipoli. He did a very brave thing last November. There was a great gas attack and he and a friend of his, Murray Sinclair, were sent up to the Front to look after the men. They had a small close dugout and over 600 men through in 3 days. They wore India rubber gloves and aprons, for this terrible new gas penetrates all clothing and it settles on the ground so you may sit down in it without knowing. It forms blisters, and one small blister will spread and spread until it covers the whole back of a man. A whiff of it getting to the lungs or stomach will in time kill a man. These two boys should have worn their gas masks, but they found this impossible in such close quarters. They got covered with steam and it was impossible to work in them, so they worked without them, at the risk of their lives, taking medicine 3 times a day. Bert has come through all right. He was examined by the doctor while he was in England, but his friend is in hospital suffering, it is feared, from tuberculosis. We may see something of him as he is at Tooting.

It was quite a long time since we have had any raids, and as we had heard that the enemy had made 17 attempts on London and had been foiled each time, we concluded that our defences were so excellent that there really was no more to fear, but last Monday and Thursday nights they visited us again. Many machines came but only a few got through. About 8.10 we heard what we thought was guns quite close, and all descended to the kitchens, but nothing more occurred and then it dawned on us that it was the warning we had heard! However, in about a quarter of an hour we heard the guns so settled ourselves in the kitchens till about 11 o'clock when all became quiet and about 12 we were all going to bed though the 'all clear' bugles had all gone, when back they came again. We descended the staircase in various stages of dishabille, when there was a violent ring at the front door. We thought it was Bert Chesters, whom we were expecting from France, but instead it was a frightened girl who had run in the interval of the guns all the way from Hampstead and was too frightened to get down to her house in Crouch End. She accompanied us to the kitchen. We got to bed finally about 1.30, after this time hearing the 'all clear'. At 3.00 Bobby began to bark violently and I went down and found it was Bert. He had been shut up for hours in Finsbury Park station and he said it was a most pathetic sight to see the little children lying about asleep. I got him some cocoa in his bedroom.

At 5 o'clock the front door bell went and Bobby barked and again I descended to find nobody there. The bell must just have sprung. While it was still dark again, the front door bell went. This time it was Hester, who had been prevented from getting here the night before.

On Tuesday evening they did not come till 10 o'clock. George was still poorly with lumbago and insisted on going to bed so I lay beside him on the bed partly dressed, but I did not like it. The guns sounded so much louder upstairs, but I was so awfully tired. I did not much mind. The others were in the kitchen, and Hester, little monkey, got quite above herself and entered into the conversation.

February 1st. Bert left by the 6.09 train on Friday morning. It was a bitterly cold foggy raw morning. His breakfast was put in his bedroom and I meant to have seen him off, but did not wake till 6.05 and heard his train go down. I was grieved, and the naughty boy had promised to call me at 5.40. He must have crept out of the house.

January 31st. Harold and Maud and he went to see *Zig Zag* on Thursday afternoon, and we had Miss Bedells in for him in the evening, so he had a good last day. The house seemed so empty yesterday with all our visitors gone. It has been so lovely to have my dear Harold. Poor Maud is very anxious about him and so are we all. We love having them here to stay. One day we went to Golders Green to choose the monument for dear Father. Harold went to the office twice and Harold Scales and

Florence treated us to lunch at the Strand Palace Hotel. Dr and Mrs Bonsfield visited us in there to tea and we had the soldier boys about all the time, but otherwise we did nothing as Harold had to be kept very quiet.

The news in the papers is very depressing. Of course it is wonderful that Jerusalem is again in the hands of Christians, but Sir Stanley Maude has died. There has been – after the wonderful victory at Cambrai, the unexplained reversion – the sinking by submarines is very heavy still week by week. The Bolsheviks are in a most dishonourable way, repudiating everything – and one thinks of what it will mean in the spring when all the men from the Eastern Front come on to the Western.

I had a very interesting letter from Millicent.

March 24th. It is a long time since I have written in this book, but I have been so frightfully busy. This is Sunday evening, and the tremendous battle which we have been anticipating began on Thursday. It is terrible. Yesterday afternoon we heard that the Germans had broken the line near St. Quentin. Today we hear that many prisoners were taken. One does not know and dare not think what may happen, but whatever the event, our men are dying now in thousands, and it is too dreadful to think of the wounded whom it is impossible to reach, and the gas. Yet everything goes on the same here, apparently, and the weather is glorious, as warm as summer, and a clear sky for days, and a brilliant moon night after night (but no raids, we wonder why). It all seems so incongruous, when there is this awful suffering so near to us. It is said today that Paris has been shelled by a tremendous gun. There is to be a special prayer meeting this evening to which all the church is asked to go.

I trust America has not come in too late. The Germans have made peace with Russia and are marching through the land as conquerors, and we are in the curious position of having been betrayed by our allies, and yet not being allowed to say anything about it because the Bolsheviks are not supposed to be the Russian people! Japan may come in to help the Allies in Siberia.

Jack left us a month ago last Friday and we had a letter from him last week posted at sea somewhere. He says the boat is most comfortable. The amputation cases have part of the deck to exercise in and he can walk now without even a stick. He was most plucky about his leg. He cut his hand very badly, falling on the platform at Blackheath, as his crutches slipped getting out of the train. He went to a doctor's and had it bound up, spent the evening at Ethel's, and had it stitched up when he got back to hospital! He could not use his crutches with this bad hand, so immediately wore his leg all day, which was very tiring for him and made him look very poorly but no doubt it made him much quicker in the use of his leg. When he went to the boat he went on his leg and sent his crutches. Most of the others, if not all, sent their legs and used their crutches. We saw him several times a week until he left and when I said goodbye to him, I was thankful it was to go back to Australia, even without a leg, rather than to go to the Front. He is a dear boy and everyone wanted to look after him, and make a fuss of him.

February 11th. He left us a legacy in the shape of his friend, Jim Gibb. The Monday before Jack left, the 'Anzac Coves' came to London from the Front to raise funds for the Australian Repatriation & Comforts Fund. They are a concert party consisting of men who have all been wounded or invalided, and they go right up to the Front to entertain the men. Some of them have been killed and on one occasion they were entertaining about 1,000 men when big shells began to fall. They continued until the tent was practically evacuated.

All the military and civilians had left the town by the next morning, but the Anzac Coves could not leave as they had not written permission. So these 8 men had the town to themselves for a week, heavily shelled every day, and one of the dresses worn by one of the 'girls' is made from a curtain from one of the wrecked houses. They took the Court Theatre for a week, and Jack went with us on Tuesday afternoon before he left to see them. He was very anxious we should ask Jim to see us, for he was very lonely and knew no one.

There was a man with a horrible big mouth – or got up to look as if he had – and I was afraid he might be Jim, but happily he wasn't! Jim came home to tea with us, to Jack's great joy, and he has been more or less with us ever since. He spent part of his furlough here, and while they are 'showing' in London makes this his headquarters. Today he has come back from Birmingham and after lunch went to bed. We shall have to wake him up for supper! He is such a fine boy, a genius, we think. He is a born actor. His recitations are wonderful, and he has very high ideals. He is the only teetotaller and non-smoker in the troupe and they treat him as their baby and would knock any man down who bothered him. He is only 21, and his range of reading is extraordinary when one thinks that he left home when he was 18. He is continually buying books which are to be sent on in relays after he goes back to France. He is keen on acting, and I have been to several 'shows' with him. *The Saving Grace* by Charles Hawtrey, *Dear Brutus* the opera, *General Post*.

Coming home from the opera we were caught in a raid. We got into the train at Covent Garden and about King's Cross I noticed some extraordinary people about. A woman in a nightgown and a jacket with her hair down her back, babies wrapped in blankets, people dressing on the platforms, and though there was no moon there was a raid warning. It turned out afterwards that there were wonderful Northern Lights – the Aurora in fact.

When we got to Finsbury Park, we could hardly get out of the train for the crowd. We hurried up onto the

GWR platform hoping to get a train to Crouch End. It was pitch dark, but just then a train did come in, into which we hopefully stepped. But there we sat, in total darkness, and then the guns began. We went into the passage and stood there for about an hour and a half with one of our choir girls whom we had come across. Then the guns ceased so we got into the train again, but there we sat in the dark and it did not start till 2.30. If we had but thought of sitting there all that time we should have walked. When we got home the house was in darkness, except for a glimmer of light in the hall. George had gone to bed and to sleep! I felt it deeply! He had got to Finsbury Park just as the warning was given and had just managed to get home before the guns had actually started much. But it was very horrid for him. But he did not worry in the least about me! I think it is partly because he hears so badly. There were some terrible bombs dropped that time, of a much heavier description.

Bert Chester's friend, Murray Sinclair, who with him so bravely attended to the gas cases in the dugout, was gassed doing it though the symptoms were not recognised at first, and he has been in a hospital at Tooting since the end of January. He has been over several times, but it takes nearly two hours to get here from Tooting, and he is very poorly still.

Dear Uncle John passed away last Wednesday week, and we went to his funeral on Monday. Auntie will feel very lonely and she is very poorly now. We cycled over to see her yesterday and the roads were so different to the last time we cycled over them, so extraordinarily free from traffic. There was hardly any.

Margaret is staying with Auntie. She had 23 letters from Frank the day before from Mesopotamia – a great accumulation of mail.

Tuesday, April 2nd. Battle of Arras. The battle raged all last week, but though our men have been pushed back a long way the line is unbroken (it was only 'pierced' at St. Quentin, not broken as reported) and the papers day after day are full of the wonderful heroism of our men. It is said that never have the German losses been so terrific, but nothing is said about ours and the Germans claim 60,000 prisoners. The French and we are working in the most absolute harmony, and today we read that the American units are to be mixed in with ours, as their 'army' is not ready to take the field yet. They have been slower in getting ready than was anticipated.

There has been no panic whatever here. In fact, one is almost tempted sometimes to wonder if the people realise what may hang on the issue of this battle. All last week we had intercession services in the church, to which hundreds came, and which Mr Ream conducted most helpfully. I have never known such an Easter. It was so quiet. The streets seemed almost empty. There could be no joy. People were asked not to travel, but many, I suppose through the result of long habit, did try to go. All had to carry their own luggage, trains were very crowded, some never got away at all, and others reached their destinations in the early hours of the morning which served them right. We went to Brathay on Easter Monday and I came back to the Red Cross sewing meeting. 2,000 bags for the soldiers (in which to put the things taken out of their pockets when they are wounded) are asked for within a fortnight. They are made of cretonne, with a plain linen patch stitched on, on which to write their names.

Compulsory rationing has been in for about a month now and is working very well. We are rationed for sugar (½ lb a head), butter or margarine 4 oz each, meat one shilling and three pence worth (which is about ¾ of a lb) and 4 oz of bacon. There are 4 coupons for meat on each card, only 3 of which can be used at the butcher's so the 5 of us put our coupons together and get a Sunday joint to the value of 6/3-, and we either get sausages or bacon with the other coupons. For 5 coupons you get 1 lb 14 oz of sausages. Of course the meat allowance is very small, but occasionally one gets a little extra. Last week I got an ox tongue without any coupon, and an extra large joint of beef, and Jim has an allowance of ½ lb a day which he does not eat all of it.

Queues have ceased now. Just before the rationing came in you would see queues of 200 or 300 people waiting to get margarine or butter. They would stand for hours. I would much rather go without, but poor people seemed as if they would wait any length of time for it. George's man, Pearce, at the office, told him how Mrs Pearce stood for hours in a queue for margarine and George said, 'We go without and eat jam,' and Pearce said, 'It may come to that with us.'

12th May. There has been a lull in the battle the last fortnight. Mount Kemmel on the Messines Ridge was taken by them, but then they had a most bloody repulse, both on our line and by the French. Every week until then they had made progress in spite of our desperate resistance, but very much slower than the first week. It did not seem to matter to them how many men they lost if they pushed us back. This was the first time that our line had absolutely held. So many of our friends have lost sons. The big gun on Paris was a fact. It shot 60 miles, and there were 3 such guns. It is said that they can only fire a very few shots before they are useless (out of action), but many people have been killed. Now, however, they seem to have ceased.

On April 17th, there was the wonderful affair at Zeebrugge when our navy, by sinking ships full of concrete, stopped the mouth of the harbour, and also damaged the 'mole'. The attempt was known to be almost certain death to the men, but 1,000 volunteered where 360 were required. It was attempted at the same time to do the same thing at Ostend, and a ship was sunk there, but owing to weather conditions, not successfully blocking the harbour. However, on the night of May 9th, another attempt was made on Ostend, and the *Vindictive* sunk right across the mouth of the harbour. Of course the Germans say no harm was done in either case, but the German submarines have had orders by wireless to return to German harbours!

We are expecting another great offensive any day. Until the last 4 or 5 days the weather has been very cold and wet. It has been impossible to give up fires, and people were going about in their fur coats. Even today we have a fire. The bad weather may have accounted for the quiet of the Germans. We quite expected at first that General Foch would make some great counter-stroke. The Germans were said to be getting themselves into a very dangerous position as regard to their flank, and General Foch (the whole of the Allied army in France is now under his command 'unity of control'. It seems an extraordinary thing that this should not have been done before) was said not to have used his reserve army, but evidently this has not been possible. The Germans, since their peace with Russia and Roumania, have brought all their divisions there onto the West Front, and our men have been fighting 1 to 3, 5 or even 7! Their heroism has been marvellous. Something happened to the Fifth Army under General Gough. He was recalled and supplanted and the significant announcement was made that for the future promotion was not to be by seniority but by recommendation or choice or something of that sort. I cannot remember the word. It was said that he drank, and that he has had warning that he refused to take notice of. Many regiments and units made the most wonderful stand individually and fought in some cases to the very last man and the situation was saved by the Third Army. French regiments fought in the same trenches with our men later, and the crisis was recognised as being so critical that America ordered her men to be interspersed among us and the French instead of going into the fight as a corporate army, as had, of course, been intended. It was very noble of America. America is said to be slow and late on the field. It is just over a year since she first declared war, but I think it is wonderful what she has done, probably, too, much more than we know.

Bernard heard the other day that the fighting men were coming over at the rate of 30,000 a week. Doctors and nurses arrived first, then a great army of transport workers and then the soldiers began to come. It seems to me that it is a triumph of shipping to bring the men in such numbers, especially under present conditions. In yesterday's paper it was announced that there are over half a million Americans in France now, and there are lots in England. It is wonderful how we can feed them all, and we are also helping France and Italy.

People are now being encouraged to keep fowls, rabbits and pigs, and Messrs McDonald Scales (George and Mr Geddes) are starting a piggery, probably at Hadley

Wood, but we shan't benefit personally by the pigs, as we shall have to use our coupons for them. We get on very well with our coupons. When a soldier – such as Jim – is with us, he gets from the Food Controllers' office in Crouch End half-pound meat coupons, for half a lb a day. With 3 of our coupons you can get little tinned lunch tongues. Now at the butcher's one may only use two coupons each a week, but each coupon is worth 6*d*, instead of 5*d*, and we may have 7 oz of bacon without bone, 8 with bone, for a coupon. It is almost impossible to get cheese, and sometimes one cannot get breakfast fish – herrings, bloaters, haddock, mackerel etc. One can always get cod at 1/10 a lb. The price for herrings etc. is 8*d* a lb. The cakes you buy now are simply horrid. No dried fruit can be got, and very little fat is used for them. Dunns cakes have dates or ginger. They are very dry. We have two cakes a week made, with ¼ lb lard – one for us, one for the kitchen, and they are quite nice. Elizabeth puts in candied peel and cherries, or ginger or caraway seeds. You can make quite nice puddings with potatoes or carrots instead of flour.

Potatoes were always supposed to make people fat, but they don't, for most people are much thinner. I have lost two stone since the war began. I don't know why. It may be the different quality of the bread that makes people thinner. We have no difficulty in getting as much milk as we want. It has gone down now from 8*d* a quart to 6*d*. One cannot get cream at all.

Clothes are most frightfully dear now, but as people are dressing very little it does not matter much. George paid 16/- wholesale for winter vests. Gabardine is 13/6 a yard. Ethel has bought a small carpet which looks like a sort of Brussels with an Axminster finish (!) in most vivid colouring for £9!

'Farringtons', Honor and Joyce's school, has been moved from Chislehurst to Bishop Teignton, on account of the raids. The school has taken 'Huntley', a Hydro, and the girls were not allowed to go home for Easter holidays, though they were allowed to go out with their parents for 10 days if they came down to them. So Ethel and Bernard went down, and Ethel stayed 3 weeks in Devonshire – part of the time with the cousins at Exmouth. It seemed rather stupid not to let the parents have the girls home if they liked, but Ethel said it was the difficulty of travelling and meeting them etc. There are fewer trains now – and much slower travelling, and 50% more costly. Hardly any luggage is allowed, yet people seem to travel more than ever.

When the great German offensive first began, conscription for men up to the age of 50 was quickly passed through Parliament. This brings in Bernard, Harold Scales and a number of our friends. Bernard is called for medical examination next week, but it is not likely that he will be called up as he is in Lloyds. The difficulties about shipping goods have become so acute that McDonald Scales and Co.'s business has practically come to a standstill. Mr Hayes leaves in a fortnight to go to temporary employment until things are better, and the staff will then consist of 3 girls and old Pearce, the odd man. The produce department has almost collapsed, too, for want of ships, so I don't know what will happen to us, but George says not to bother at all at present, as such unlooked for things do happen.

Alice has decided to leave, on account of her health. I shall miss her dreadfully. She wants a very light place, as housekeeper or useful maid, and has been to see ever so many ladies, but all seem to be reducing their establishments and wanting to get a great deal of work out of the girls they have. She is going away for a fortnight next week, and then will return to us for the month of June, unless she hears of anything which just suits her. I had quite decided, if she left, to manage with two maids, but Elizabeth is too old to do much more work than she is doing, and Rhodes too young, and I find I shall need so much extra help that the expense would not be much less. Also, visitors would then be a great difficulty and we do not want to give up having our soldiers unless we are obliged.

February 17th. Arthur Brooker, son of Mr Brooker of Crookes & Brooker, at Adelaide, stayed with us from Cheltenham. A very nice, simple-minded boy, quiet and shy except when you have him by himself. He had had a shot through his leg, which made his foot go flop, and it was fastened up to his knee with a little strap and chain. He had leave from hospital, and then went to Weymouth and from there, to his great joy, was sent back to Adelaide.

Murray Sinclair came out to see us several times, but he was very ill. The last time he came, I walked down to the station with him and had no idea till then how bad he was. He was moved from Tooting to Harefield, and George cycled over to see him one day and took me over last Wednesday week, 2nd May. When we got to Denham, there was no bus to Harefield but a man took us in a car. It is an enormous hospital of large wooden huts, holding 1,500 men. Murray was delighted to see us and we had tea with him in the canteen and got back in time for the Home Missionary meeting at Westminster. He was expecting to be sent off almost directly to Australia, and promised to write to tell us, but we have not heard from him and I don't understand it.

Jim is still with us. He has been to Liverpool, Manchester, Glasgow, had another week in London at the Ambassador's, a week at Wimbledon, and at Hammersmith. Last week he was at Bournemouth, Portsmouth and Croydon. While he was at Wimbledon, Hammersmith, the Ambassador's and Croydon he came home to sleep, arriving often very late. We let him have the key which was very good of George, and he had supper when he came in. I don't like the life for him at all and he is not looking at all well. But one is very thankful for him to be out of France, and we shall feel dreadfully parting with him next Wednesday, to go back. He writes, and reads us his compositions. He always looks very nice. He is a good looking boy, with very thick black hair and very amusing.

It is very wonderful how the money for our campaign comes in answer to prayer. When we pray, it comes; when we don't it doesn't come. At our W.A. meeting I was able to announce £11,150 in promises of £100 or over, but we see great difficulties before us for our annual income. Exchange in China is so bad, that for every £100 we used to send we have now to send £150.

Guy Wagg, who stayed with us last August, came back from France and came up to see us. He spent a Saturday with us, then went up to Glasgow to the 'Overseas' Club where Jim stayed, and where the ladies were awfully good to him. He is now at Sling Camp, having such a poor time that he thinks of asking to go back to France again!

We have not yet heard of Jack's arrival in Australia, but we had a cable and a letter from Cape Town, and we think he must have arrived safely by now.

I had a letter from Bert Chesters yesterday saying the following:

We have some pleasures out here, as lately we have been sleeping in double beds, with soft mattresses and clean sheets, which were left behind by the fleeing inhabitants.

'Tis a cruel waste, and I do pity them very much. It has its humorous side, in that in the deserted villages were found stacks of civilian clothing, and it was the funniest sight on earth to see some of our boys with dress suits, top hats and walking sticks parading about.

Gainor Jackson, the brother of Alban and Ernest, spent an evening with us on February 22nd. He is a very clever boy, an officer, and gave us most interesting details on tactics etc. He went to France in March and on April 9th I had a letter from him.

October 24th. I have written nothing in this book since 12th May, and since then we have had a great sorrow. Our darling Mother left us in the early morning of June 25th. I will not write about it here. She was only taken ill at 9.20 on the Monday evening, and died at 3 o'clock on Tuesday morning. George and I got down at 11.30 and we watched her peacefully passing away. I was so thankful that there was no raid. Friday, the day we laid her to rest, was a beautiful day and as we stood round her grave, the sun shining and everything looking so peaceful, the great guns at Woolwich were booming.

I so wish she had heard news from the Front such as we are having now. The war weighed upon her very heavily, and made her very sad. She felt the pain and sorrow and suffering caused by it so keenly, but she was always so calm and quiet. She never got up during raids, just stayed in her bed in the dining room, looking so peaceful, and when she had visitors staying with her like Aunt Jennie or Mrs Kenyon, they used to come down and sit by her fire until the raid was over, and Miss Davis would get them something warm to drink. Miss D. herself would not have got up at all, and did not much like people coming into the room. For one thing, I don't think she liked being seen with all her curlers in, but it was a very good thing she was so calm and collected. (Maud, going to rouse Mrs Kenyon who is rather deaf, one night in a raid, found her asleep, with her transformation lying on the pillow beside her.)

Maud and Harold spent the whole of the winter with Mother, so she was not lonely. They have let their house, and Maud does not mean to return to housekeeping until the war is over, a resolution caused by 3 considerations, I think:

1. The nearness of their house to the river
2. The difficulty of getting maids
3. The difficulty of getting food

They are staying on at Brathay till the middle of December, and then the two maids are to go to Ethel, for Ethel's Francis has left to go on the land – dear old Ellen is retiring, after about 40 years of faithful service in the Matthews' family, and Mabel, who came to Mother direct from school and has been with Ethel since her marriage, has been seized with the general feeling of unrest, and is leaving. I have had rather a disturbed time with maids, but have been more fortunate than most. The day I came home from Brathay after dear Mother's departure, Alice left in the evening to go to her new place as companion help, and in the evening George came home with flu. I only had Rhodes at home as Elizabeth was not returning from her holiday for 5 days, and I spent the day running up and downstairs trying to cook for George and I can't cook, and neither could Rhodes. It was really most trying that he was ill just then.

On the Saturday, Mrs Norman Sargant had a sale for church funds in her garden, and wanted me to help in spite of our sorrow, because so many people had failed her.

Everyone now is engaged in war work, or housework for want of maids. A Mrs Murray, the wife of a sergeant at the Front, who is the sister of Mrs Burton who lives in the other half of 'Crouchman's', offered to come to us as parlour maid. She came, and I like her very much personally, and am very glad to have had her, but I doubt if she will stay long as she has not been used to our kind of situation and finds the work hard. She was head nurse to the Countess of Leicester.

However, Alice has come back in a new capacity, as 'useful maid', or 'assistant housekeeper', and I am delighted to have her back, and hope she will find she can manage the work.

I think I will write about the war situation at the moment, before trying to write up the events of the last few months.

On Sunday, October 7th (or 8th) we heard that Germany had sent a 'peace note' to President Wilson. This we could hardly believe, but during the week following, the news of victory upon victory was in the papers. One day (October 17th) in the one paper was 'Ostend, Lille and Donai all taken by the Allies'. Then came the evacuation of the Belgian coast and Bruges and further advance south. (They did not get to Valenciennes till November 2nd. Gainor said that just as our offensive was to have begun, the Germans launched a big one, which deferred ours.)

Yesterday we read of a 'Great British Advance' in the neighbourhood of Valenciennes, on a 20-mile front, and see a letter received from Gainor Jackson yesterday. There are also hints of disturbances in Germany (though we are sceptical of these stories now) and Prince Max is supposed to represent government by the German people. But President Wilson sees through their strategy (political) and in today's paper (October 25th) his reply is that he has submitted the request for an armistice to the Allies, but that the only one he can agree to will be a surrender, unless the government of Germany is radically altered – he will not treat with the Kaiser, 'as his word cannot be relied on', only with the people.

One knows that our successes are brought at a terrible price, and we long for peace, but it must be a peace that will ensure peace to our children. There has been comparatively little rejoicing about the request for an armistice, for everyone distrusts every move of the Germans, but if only there <u>could</u> be peace!

The evacuation of the Belgian coast probably means there will be no more air raids over London and the east coast, for which one would be very thankful – as the base will have to be so far away. The accounts in the papers of the reception of the Allies at Lille and the villages round, and Ostend, are pathetic, but before these towns, and Bruges, were evacuated, all males from 15 to 60 were marched off – no one knows whither. The stories of the trials the people have borne are terrible and the Huns are devastating the towns and country, though this has ceased somewhat since the German peace note, and President Wilson's reply that these atrocities and submarine atrocities must cease before an armistice could be considered.

Just after the peace note was sent, the *Leinster* was sunk – the Irish packet – and hundreds of people drowned. No such indignation has been aroused since the sinking of the *Lusitania*. It was a cruel, wicked thing.

The treatment of our prisoners is dreadful too, and one trembles for our men. Many have been killed through neglect and cruelty, and the accounts given by the English colony in Lille as to the way British prisoners were treated makes one's blood run cold. It seems, as we have so many more prisoners than they have, that we ought to be able to stop it. We think of Rod Piper at 'Gustrow' on the Baltic, a splendid boy from Adelaide, who went out full of enthusiasm. When letters do come, of course they are censored, and nothing can be put in them. We read of our men in mines, starved, in dangerous places just behind the German lines, neglected in illness, and one very much fears for them – an added fear – now that this peculiar sort of influenza is rampant, which leads to pneumonia. It is <u>sure</u> to be fatal to many. It is too awful, and it seems as if <u>nothing</u> can be done! One thinks very much about our men, too, with this epidemic. In one evacuated town in the paper yesterday, it said that 1,500 civilians were suffering with this influenza and were down in the cellars. The Germans knew the conditions, but deliberately shelled the town during the night, and many died. And it will be impossible for soldiers to lay up at once. The only hope is that they are in such a fit condition that they will resist its attack.

Gainor's letter is wonderfully hopeful and one trusts his hopes may prove correct. He is a very wise and clever boy, and has, of course, inside knowledge. If so, we may hope for great results from this latest great British advance. But he is in the line again, and I see from the paper this morning that the New Zealanders have been heavily engaged south of Valenciennes and it makes one very anxious about him.

George wrote this morning saying that a cable had come from New Zealand saying that he has been recommended for exemption. His two brothers, Ernest and Alban, have both been killed. I have written about Alban's visit to us with his bride. He went to New Zealand to bring troops home and after that had a very happy time with his wife on Salisbury Plain. He had only been back at the Front 10 days when he was killed. Gainor sent us word of Ernest's death one day, and Alban's the next, within about 4 miles of each other.

It is very pathetic. They were both fine men. Alban was about 27 and Ernest 29 years old. Ernest was engaged to a Miss Kate Bond at Auckland. He told me all about her one evening when George was out, and showed me her first letter to him which was almost worn out with constant folding and unfolding. He wrote to me to tell me that Gainor was engaged to 'the prettiest girl in the North Island', and then added, 'Never mind, all is not gold that glitters,' by which I gathered that Miss Bond is not beautiful! He stayed with us two nights, I think, and came over again with a friend. He was quite a character. He told me he thought I was a 'fine woman'. I don't think the poor fellow had talked to a British woman for months. Mr Jackson, the father, died in the spring and poor Mrs Jackson is a widow with some young children, and a cripple daughter. Gainor, aged 25, is now the head of the family. There is a boy of 20 in camp. Gainor ought to have had leave some time ago, but he can't be spared.

I do hope he will be kept safe. He is a very clever boy, and his great idea in his leave is to give his poor sister-in-law a good time. We have asked her to stay with us when he comes back.

George and I came to Scarborough on October 10th. He had only had a week's holiday this year, except the public holidays, and I had got suddenly thin which had upset the family, but I don't think it is to be wondered at, what with rations, and other things. We stayed until October 21st (dear Mother's birthday) in rooms that Con had got for us – 23 Esplanade Gardens, where the whole family of us stayed 13 years ago. Con had put flowers in the room, and brought in all sorts of provisions, and we saw a lot of her and on October 21st I came on to her and Mrs Raynor at Normanton Rise, and hope to stay until October 30th, unless George gets this influenza. We were afraid we should have a very crowded journey up, and got to King's Cross about an hour before the train was timed to start, but the carriage only had 6 people in it. (You can't get anything to eat anywhere.)

Percy met us at York and we had no trouble at all anywhere. The streets are very dark here, and the windows most carefully curtained. It is extraordinary to see how close the German ships came in when they bombarded Scarborough 4 years ago. A good swimmer could have swum out to them, and if they had been further out they would have done more damage. As it was, many of the shells flew over the town. Con had shrapnel in her room, and it seems marvellous that <u>more</u> damage was not done, though a great deal <u>was</u> done.

Con and I went out to coffee one evening with some friends of Con's (a young South African was there) and it was so pitch dark that if you had turned round you would not know which way to walk.

George went to Whitby and he and I to Bridlington, but it is impossible to do many excursions and there are so few trains now. The town is bursting with soldiers. At the time of the bombardment there was not a gun or soldiers in the place. They are billeted in empty houses, unfurnished, and it must be most comfortless for them. At South Cliff chapel there is a splendid canteen for them. George spoke to the men on the two Sunday nights he was here, and the first night a soldier stopped him and asked him if he was a minister, and told him his wife was to have an operation that day and he had had to leave her, and asked him to pray for her. So George took him into our rooms. I went on Monday night to help Con wash up, and the men seemed to be having quite a good time. Most of them went to France last night. Every day we used to see them march past, hundreds of them, with a band, and the Colonel riding on a white horse. They do physical drill opposite the house in the road often, and they drill on the beach too. The men are billeted in the houses. There is no furniture whatever, only their beds, and they look most comfortless. I suppose it would cost a great deal to furnish them, for furniture now is an incredible price. Quinton sold all his, bought about 25 years ago, for more than he gave for it then. Still, the Government cares so little what it spends, that one would think a little furniture might be provided.

This is a true story I heard the other day. A man had been taken for the army from an engineering firm to which he was of great value. Eventually the firm got him back, under the proviso that he was only to receive army pay. After a year, they represented to the Government that he deserved higher pay, and suggested £150 a year. The Government agreed, and £150 arrived the first month, £150 the second, £150 the third. The firm pointed out that a mistake was being made, but they were told to 'mind their own business', and the same rate of pay is still going on. The firm is putting it in the bank in case they should have to refund. It is the same with munition workers. Mere boys are often paid £3 a week – maid servants go to pay offices at the same rates. This of course raises wages all round and it is very hard on the small businesses. The Government has appealed to the cupidity of the nation instead of to its patriotism. At Harold's pay office he said that 3 trained men could easily have done the work of the 20 untrained women.

December 4th. Again there is a long gap since I last wrote in this book, and most wonderful things have happened.

The last few days of my stay in Scarborough, Austria sued for peace [27 October] and the Italians advanced driving a disorganised foe before them. Our army was a great help to them. The Serbians reached the Danube on October 29th, and the Turks were granted an armistice on the 30th. The successes came on all fronts with a great rush, and looking back a year it seems too wonderful to be true. On November 30th 1917 we had our disaster at Cambrai. February 1st, Germany's peace with the Ukraine and [they] invade[d] Russia. Then came the Brest Treaty. February 9th, whatever people say about the poor Czar, Russia was faithful to the Allies while he was in power, and since his enforced abdication she has been false to all her pledges. On March 21st, the great German offensive in the West began and until 21st May, day after day we read of retreat and towns lost. The Germans got again very near to Paris. We held them on 21st May, there was another great offensive on June 9th, when again they advanced, but were held sooner, and another on July 15th where again they advanced, but with less vigour each time, and our power of holding them was greater.

Everyone knew that this was the most critical time in the war since August 1914, and very great anxiety was felt, but there was no panic. There were intercession services everywhere. 15,000 volunteers were asked for for the east coast, to set free 15,000 soldiers, for every man was needed. Bernard went and was near the Norfolk Broads. He was there 2 months and came home splendidly fit, but the work and training had been very rigorous. We expected him to be called up the day after dear Mother's funeral, but fortunately it was not till a week later. There was another great comb out in the trades and government departments and men were called up for medical examination again.

It seemed as if <u>nothing</u> could resist the onward rush of the Germans. They came in such great masses that our men could not withstand them. They seemed absolutely regardless of life. Of course we know now that it was their last great effort. That they knew that if they could not get to Paris then their doom was sealed. But of course we did not know this.

On June 23rd came the news of the great Austrian defeat, but we did not realise the significance of it, and only said, 'It isn't Germany.' Meanwhile, America had acted nobly. Such of her men as were in France she placed entirely at General Foch's disposal [he was made 'Generalissimo' on April 14th]. At the beginning of the German offensive she had not many, she had been so slow in getting them, but now they began to come over in huge convoys. When I was in Liverpool about July 16th, Mr Davison rang up one morning to say that a huge convoy had come up the Mersey. Mabel and I went down and took a ferry boat and saw these great ships (one of them was the *Aquitania*), packed with the long-legged, khaki-clad Americans, up the rigging, and in every square inch of space. There were about 22,000 men in that convoy, and they were coming to Liverpool in two and three such convoys a week and to other ports as well – Bristol for one. And it had all been kept so quiet. It was not generally known at all. The ships were camouflaged and looked so strange. Instead of the Americans going in to fight as one army, they were distributed among British and French, and boys from the Front told us that this had put wonderful heart into our men – the new gay blood coming in when they were so desperately war weary. It was the same with the French. The French and the British were put together too. This was part of General Foch's plan, and worked splendidly. Our men were delighted with the Americans, only they said they were too reckless, just as our men were at the beginning, and had to learn their lesson by bitter experience.

December 7th. After all these weeks of retreat and loss, on July 18th General Foch's counter attack began, and here we really heard of the Americans for the first time, and were delighted with their fighting spirit. The big salient towards Paris was gradually reduced and 'pinched off'. The Germans were forced back across the Marne. Soisson was recovered on August 2nd, and from then onwards, victory followed victory. On September 27th, the dreaded Hindenburg line, which the Germans thought impregnable, was broken.

On September 29th, Bulgaria surrendered, and this began the break up. In 5 weeks enemy governments and armies all crumbled up and fell to pieces. It was like a miracle. I should say, it <u>was</u> a miracle.

On July 15th, they still seemed irresistible.

Less than 4 months later, Germany sued for peace – the last of our enemies.

The Palestine and Mesopotamian victories had no doubt much to do with our victory in the West. When Jerusalem was taken on December 9th, 1917, everyone was delighted but more from a religious and romantic standpoint, but we did not properly grasp the importance of this Eastern campaign, or its influence on the West. But when Turkey was conquered, and Bulgaria, then Germany's back door was closed, and Austria was hampered. This is what politicians were looking for in the Gallipoli campaign. No doubt both these campaigns were very ably conducted and they are a brilliant story to read.

I came home from Scarborough on October 30th, little thinking how near we were to peace. I had rather dreaded the journey, for I was not very well and was afraid I might not get a seat in the train at York. However, Percy most kindly met me (bringing me a little bottle of cream! You can't get cream for love or money without a doctor's certificate) and I got a corner seat in the train. The corridor was full of soldiers who were too shy to take a seat that was to spare. There was a wounded soldier, so I asked him if he would not come in. He looked very shy and said, 'No,' so I said, 'Do,' and he said, 'I can't sit down' (I didn't believe it). There were two charming Irish girls in my carriage. Their husbands were officers travelling first class, and they got one to come in, but he sat, very red, on the edge of the seat, and I caught winks between him and his friends.

There were no porters at King's Cross, and it was very dark, but fortunately I had sent on my box, and only had portable luggage. Presently I saw George tear past me full-speed looking ahead. I shouted to him – of course he did not hear, and I had to run after him at the peril of losing my luggage.

All sorts of rumours now began to fly about. Famine in Germany, disaffection in the armies and mutiny in the German fleet, but there have been so many rumours that we believed none of them. At the end of the October, the Germans asked for an armistice, and that hostilities might cease during the consideration of the terms. This last request was refused, and everyone much hoped that the German army would be thoroughly conquered before the terms were arranged and General Foch <u>did</u> go ahead. It was thrilling day after day to read the papers.

When the terms were declared on November 4th, everyone was delighted, for we had had a sort of fear that we might be too lenient. Now we thought it was almost impossible for the enemy to accept them.

On Thursday, November 7th, Mr Arthur Dixon rang up to say that he would like to come to us for Sunday, but he might be kept at the Home Office. No one knew what might happen. He also said that it was quite expected that the German Fleet would come out, and there would be a great battle. Most people thought there would be some great German coup or display at the end, and Mr Dixon could not come. People had the feeling that anything might happen, but our daily life went on just as usual.

On Saturday, November 9th, the German envoys arrived in the French lines with their <u>white flag</u>. I hope one day some poet will depict that wonderful historic scene. The proud overbearing insulting cruel Germans arriving horribly with only 4 of them – with a white flag, the emblem of defeat and petition. Sunday was a day of quiet thanksgiving, for though the armistice was not yet signed and we did not feel as if it <u>could</u> be – yet we knew Germany must be at her last gasp to take any such step as she had already taken. Ethel and Bernard were with us, and we were very happy. In the evening, Gainor Jackson rang up. He had come straight from France, and he said that, as he left, the day before the Canadians had got into Mons! It was so wonderful, such historic and romantic justice. One's thoughts went back to the glorious Retreat from Mons and on the day before the armistice was signed, Mons is ours again.

How many times in this war one sees the hand of God, and words cannot express the wonder and gratitude one feels in the answers that have come to our prayers, and as one thinks of it one can only say, 'O Lord, we thank Thee, and may we use this victory Thou has given us to right old wrongs and to make the world a better and purer place for Thy spirit to work in.'

Gainor had been in the thick of the fighting. Of 42 officers in his battalion only 2 remained, of whom he is one. He said that peace <u>must</u> come and that the Germans were simply crumpling up, either running away or running towards them with hands held up, shouting 'Kamerade'. That behind their lines was most utter confusion, and this we had heard from the papers. He had got home 2 days in advance of his leave because he had great luck. Soon after he left the lines, he saw a motor car, and stopped it and asked if it would give him a lift. It turned out to be a General's car, with the General inside, and he took him ever so far on his way. Then when he got to the quay, a steamer was just leaving for England, and he just had time to rush on board. He was very well and naturally in great spirits.

November 11th. The next morning, Monday, we all wondered what we should hear, but really people could not believe that they would hear that the armistice was signed. The Barry family were down with influenza – 6 of them, so Ethel and I started out to take them 2 quarts of Bengers food. It was very sloppy! Just as we got to the door of what we thought was their house (though we had got the wrong address) an old man came up the steps and he said, 'I wonder if those guns mean peace.' We had heard no guns, but just at that moment bang went a maroon somewhere near. There were shrieks, and flying feet, and the street was cleared in the twinkling of any eye. People thought it was an air raid. Then more maroons went, and we knew it was 'peace' at last. Ethel and I knew it must be so directly the maroon went at 10.52 a.m. In a very few minutes windows were thrown open, doors flew open and people crowded to the doors and windows. A few called to us, for I think we were the only people out, 'Is it an air raid?' and we called, 'It's peace, peace.' Flags suddenly appeared from windows and everyone began to laugh and talk, and the children to dance. It was a very poor neighbourhood we were in, Pemberton Gardens, Junction Road, Up. Holborn.

I had an appointment with the dentist at 12.30 to have gas so Ethel and I speeded on to Shoolbred's to get flags.

Tottenham Court Road was crowded with people, hands out of shops and factories, girls arm in arm, a dozen abreast, dancing down the roads, cheering and surrounding every wounded soldier, hundreds of little flags being waved and trains and buses decorated with them. There were heaps of flags in Shoolbred's flag department, strewn all over the floor, but an awful price and everyone saying different prices. We got a few and then went on to the dentist's. It really was very trying to have to go there, and then we came straight home. I was very sorry for Ettie that we could not do anything.

When we got home we found our big flags hung out across the garden and Guy and Gainor had both rung up saying they would be down to tea. I did not feel as jolly as I would have liked, but it was very nice to have the boys. Guy had given his men a holiday till 8 o'clock, and then found they had gone into public houses near, so he routed them out, and told them if they were going to do that they should come back to work again. George also got home to tea. He had gone to St Giles's at 11 o'clock, and found people pouring into the church for an impromptu thanksgiving service, and there were services there all the morning. There had been an impromptu great thanksgiving service in St Paul's at 12 noon. In the evening our missionary meeting was turned into a thanksgiving service, and all that people could say to each other was, 'Isn't it wonderful!' It was so great that everything seemed banal.

Gainor had brought most interesting maps home – some German ones – and he gave George some for souvenirs. We spent a good part of the evening looking at them. Eth went with George to the service. The next day I had to go to bed for my month's rest cure for my heart. It was rather trying that it should have happened just then, for Ethel and I might have gone about and entered into the public rejoicings. As it was, the darling would stay with me. The King and Queen drove about London, different directions on different days, receiving tremendous ovations everywhere. Ethel went to the chapel to see them pass one day that week and George had all our flags there, so we had nothing to decorate our own house with! There was a great thanksgiving service on Sunday, November 17th, in St Paul's, and churches everywhere were crowded, queues in many places. When the King and Queen reviewed the silver badge men, after 1 side of the 3 sides of the square had been reviewed the men made a rush at the King and the royal carriage and shook his hand and went quite mad. St James's Park is full of German guns, unguarded, and the children play all over them.

The next day, November 12th, the order for shading lights was removed, so now one does not have to carefully close up every chink round the windows at a stated time, or see that one's blinds are carefully drawn. It is such a relief. Also, the lamps that are allowed in the streets are clear, which makes the streets much lighter, though the full number of lamps is not allowed because of the shortage of coal. Also, every bang one hears after dark one need not think, 'Is that a gun?', 'Is there an air raid?' though still one's thoughts do fly that way at every unusual sound. I think there are no other practical changes yet.

The food situation is much the same, and is not likely to vary much at present, nor are prices expected to come down much yet, but – the war is over!

I think the treatment by the Germans of our prisoners of war has made one feel more furious with the Huns, the brutes, than anything else. To think that men, supposed to be civilised, could treat other men in their power – defenceless, ill, wounded – as they have treated our men, seems impossible and unthinkable. Today, George went to King George's Hospital to see Rod Piper. He is the son of a lawyer in Adelaide, and is a private in the Australian army. He was so delighted when he was last here on October 25th, 1917, that he was going out to France directly. He is about 20 years old, I think. He was taken prisoner on April 5th of this year, and was reported to be at Güstrow Gefangenenlager and his parcels were sent there, two a week. But he was never there, and all the time has been working just behind the German lines, so the Germans have been eating his food. A cousin of Bernard's, Tonkin, was reported to be in the same camp, and was never there. He has just arrived in England too. Rod arrived in this hospital on Thursday, and is coming here as soon as he can, so I will not write about his experiences till I hear them from himself.

Harry Brooker was taken prisoner just a year ago. He was wounded, and lay out two days before the Germans got him in, and machine guns played all round him. It was a miracle that his life was spared. He is an officer, and was not badly treated in hospital. He was first at Aachen and was then taken onto Heidelberg. There, if you went for a walk at all, it was always about 7 miles, and the men were not equal to it, so Harry only went once I think. His arm did not get well, so he applied to go to Holland for treatment, and to his great surprise was sent there. In Germany, his food was black bread and soup made of potatoes and carrot, twice a day, and the men would have starved if it had not been for their parcels. Though Harry was 5 months in Germany, he did not get any parcels till the day he was leaving, when he had two, but the men who had been imprisoned a long time shared their food with him. That was the way they did with newcomers.

The French and Italians were much worse off than the British and there was a receptacle in which the British used to put what they could spare for the other nationalities. This was generally oxo and dripping, and one day someone wrote on the tin, 'Man cannot live by oxo and dripping only.' There were two Serbian colonels in his camp.

He gave us an extraordinary account of how prisoners sometimes escaped by digging a tunnel. The first difficulty was what to do with the earth, and the men would take it out in their pockets and scatter it about the yard. Then they had to obtain an extra suit for digging in so that there might be no earth stains on their clothes. As the tunnel progressed, it had to be bricked up and this they did with German bread which in 3 days is as hard as a brick. Then they had to make a compass to tell the direction in which to work, get wire to electrify it and run it along the tunnel to be able to work. They got fresh air into the tunnel by means of condensed milk tins stuck together. The opening they used if possible to get in a clump of bushes, and this had to be selected and worked towards on one of their walks. The distance being paced. When they thought they had reached the clump, they would put a wire through the ground and then they started to break through this last bit of ground. As many as 40 men have escaped like this at once, but about half are always recaptured. The rations they take with them if possible are uncooked bacon and chocolate, as being the most sustaining. This would take many months to prepare, and they would have to get civilian clothes to take with them.

Another way he told us was to make German uniforms, dummy bayonets, caps etc. but this was equally difficult in another way. Then the 2 pseudo German officers, with 3 or 4 prisoners, would march boldly up to the gate, give the word of command, the gates would be opened and they would be free.

He told us too of a society in London which makes plans for prisoners to escape. Directions are sent in all sorts of secretive ways, rolled up in a prune after the stone is extracted, rolled up in a cigarette, with tobacco both ends, in the binding of a book. If a tin was marked 'not to be opened till used' they knew there was some tool, or something of that sort inside it, and would smuggle it out if possible, as all tins had to be opened before a German.

Harry was pretty well. In Holland he had lived in an hotel and had been there for 7 months. He had lived on boiled fish and just before dinner said he loathed fish! It was fortunate he said so, as I had fish for dinner, though it was fried! I hurriedly substituted ox tail. The allowance of meat in Holland was 1 oz a week. He thinks the food conditions here are wonderful. We get about ¾ lb of meat a person a week, and sausages and bacon are both uncouponed now, also this week the coupons have been taken off tongues, kidneys etc. Tripe has been uncouponed for some time. Fruit, fresh or dried, is unobtainable and has been for months. Apples have been 1/6 and 2/6 a lb! No fruit could be got in the summer. It was a very bad year and all the fruit there was was commandeered for the army. Mr and Mrs Geddes sent me 25 lbs of blackberries from 'Crouchman's'.

December 16th. I went to see a specialist, Dr Percy Kidd, last Thursday and he says I am to give up all work of every kind, mental and physical, and live a lazy life for, probably, several years, but I think, if I do it properly, I shall be all right in a year. But it is trying to do nothing these tremendously interesting years.

Last Thursday, 12th, Gainor Jackson and Lieut. Clarence Lane from Whangaroa came to dinner to say goodbye (Guy Wagg came too). They are expecting to be off to New Zealand this week. It is said that 16 boats are sailing before the end of the year. Clarence Lane had been shot by the same bullet in both arms. It had gone through one arm, hit on the metal of his gas mask, buried itself in his right arm, the nerves of which it had shattered. But power was gradually coming back and he could use somewhat all his fingers but 2.

Our navy has reaped the reward of its wonderful silent work on the sea. The German fleet surrendered in the North Sea the week after the Armistice was signed, and the submarines gave themselves up at different ports until their full number, 150 (?), was complete. 209 have been destroyed by our methods. It is said that the German envoy objected to the demand for the surrender of the fleet, on the grounds that the fleet had not been beaten, to which Admiral Wemyss replied, 'It had only to come out.' Our army now occupies Cologne, and in today's paper it said that the Cologne papers have printed on the top 'printed by permission of the British'.

But internal affairs in Germany seem in a very uncertain state and the consensus of opinion in the papers is that Germany does not understand yet that it is beaten. Berlin has given a flourishing welcome to its soldiers.

President Wilson arrived in France on Friday, and had a tremendous welcome in Paris on Saturday. One wonders what his attitude will be at the Peace Conference.

Food conditions are already getting rather easier. We are to have an extra quarter of a lb of sugar now, and all insides of animals can be bought without coupons. Dear old Hugo has sent us 5 lbs of butter from Australia, and Maud tea, sugar and chocolate butter, and Dolly sugar. It is all a great help. Guy brought me 4 lbs of currants, 2 lbs of raisins.

Frank Brown is a New Zealander who has been to see us several times, and Flo most kindly took him when I was having my rest cure. He has been a B.3 man for months. When there was the 'disaster' at Cambrai in April he was in hospital in France with mumps. Word was sent up that every man who was out of bed was to be hurried into the line. Frank had just got out of bed that day and he was sent up. The consequence was that in 5 days he was very ill, and has been in convalescent camps ever since. The boys last Thursday night were talking about Cambrai. They said it was nobody's fault. They did not blame General Gough as he was blamed here. They said that an attack in force was not expected there, that the reserves were at two other parts of the line. That the whole front was riddled with spies. That a 'brigadier general' was in the rear sending trains <u>back</u> full of the reinforcements (he was shot), that officers everywhere were ordering the men to retreat and when one division had retreated – instructed by these false officers – others had necessarily to fall back. That at last instructions were sent that every officer who ordered men to retreat was to be shot at once, unless he was personally known. Guy said that when he came home in April he was most pessimistic. That our men were so sick of the war they would have been glad to be conquered. He had been at the 'cleaning up' after the Cambrai business.

George Bottoms came to see us in the summer and he had the Military Cross for his actions at Cambrai. He said the confusion was awful. Germans before and behind them. He and some of his men fought their way back to a village and there he went to find some headquarters for instructions and lost his men. He found that a part of the line had none guarding it, about 600 yards, and no soldiers behind either. He managed to collect about 300 or 400 men who had lost their officers, all sorts of regiments, and manned the line – several yards between each two men and this they held for two days without relief, he and a 2nd Lieutenant being senior officers. If the Germans had known, they could just have poured through. There was nothing to stop them. This war has been full of miracles. After two days an officer and men appeared, understanding that that portion of the line was unoccupied and quite surprised to find them there. All the boys the other night said that all our line consisted of very strong frontal defence, but nothing in the rear, so that if these frontal defences could be pierced and the men got behind them, we had nothing to fall back on. This was very different to what we had been told – <u>miles</u> of fortified and entrenched ground – in depth I mean. It seemed very risky.

Of course these were New Zealanders talking but they all agreed that the Tommies were splendid, but that some of the regiments were very badly officered.

George was counting up the other day. We have had 57 soldiers in our house, many of them for long visits.

Two of our New Zealand boys were killed in August – Ernest Jackson on the 3rd, Alban Jackson on the 9th. Poor Gainor wrote to tell us. His father had died in the spring. Alban's wife was expecting a baby, and was terribly distressed, and had a miscarriage. He was a fine young fellow. Ernest was older and was engaged to a New Zealand girl, Kate Bond.

The last raid we had was on Whit Sunday. George and I were at Crouchman's Farm, 36 miles from London. I woke up in the night hearing the guns, and felt sure it was a raid on London and sometimes the cottage shook with the bombs. It lasted a long time, and it was dreadful to hear it at that distance. I did not wake George. The next morning George could not get a paper, but he heard there had been a raid, and that an aeroplane had been brought down. There was a thrilling fight in the air over London. We cycled out to Danbury that day and heard more from a soldier. A living and a dead German prisoner had just gone through the little town (or village) in a car. An aeroplane had been brought down at Burnham on Crouch. A great deal of damage was done in South London and Hither Green, but it was always very difficult to find out where damage had been done. The papers never published it.

Last Saturday, December 11th, we had the parliamentary elections – very historical ones, for they were the first at which women have had a vote, and so much depends on them because of the Peace terms, and economic conditions now the war is over. The parties in England are: the Coalition (Lloyd George), Independents and Liberals (Mr Asquith) and Labour. Our member, Coalition, was returned unopposed, so I did not vote. One would have voted for Lloyd George, of course, because he will be sound on peace terms, and Mr Asquith cannot be trusted, but one is anxious about what he may do in other directions and we doubt if he is a man to be trusted in other lines. We shall see, and there are sure to be very difficult, anxious, and perhaps very perilous days before us. But the war is over, and what else matters!

Norman Sargant stood for North Islington as a Liberal but had no chance. I think he and Mrs Norman are awfully disappointed. He only just escaped, if he <u>did</u> escape, a fine for not polling a certain proportion of the votes polled – I think an eighth. The Coalition man got in with a huge majority and the Labour man was next. The Sargants were grieved that their friends had not helped more, but most of them are not Norman's politics. I was glad the Coalition man got in, but sorry for the Sargants. I never thought Norman sound on the war. He did nothing to help until he was forced under the Conscription Act. He managed to keep out of serving, but began to learn motor driving and met the soldiers at stations and then went everywhere in his volunteer uniform. Lived in it, I think.

Guy's story, January 19th, 1919
Dictated by him on a Sunday evening:

Had completed five years as a territorial when the war broke out (under the Compulsory Service Act in New Zealand). I joined the army on August 13th, 1914, in Wanganui. I was discharged from the Expeditionary Force on October 1st, and sailed as ship's engineer because an engineer could not be got to work the ship, the *Arawa*. We laid in Wellington till October 15th. During that time the *Scharnhörst* and *Gneisenau* were seen off the Heads, or we would have sailed earlier. There were 11 ships in the NZ convoy. We proceeded to Hobart, escorted by the Japanese cruiser *Hibooki*, two ships of the NZ navy, *Psyche* and *Pyramus*. We moved off at 6 o'clock in the morning and hardly a soul knew we were going. We went ashore at Hobart and marched round and had a tremendous welcome. Tons of apples were put onboard for the troops, who did not have them. From there we went to Albany and picked up 38 Australian transports. We did not go ashore, but there was huge excitement, and the *Sydney* and the *Brisbane* and another Japanese boat were added to the escort. These were escorting the Australians.

We were sailing for Cape Town as far as we could tell and went in that direction for 48 hours and then headed due north and sailed straight for Colombo. Forty-eight hours' sail from Colombo we received the SOS message from Kokos Island [Guy's ship was the only one that picked it up] stating that the *Emden* had destroyed their wireless plant. The ship received SOS SO (chopped off then). The *Sydney* then left us and went to the rescue of the wireless operators on the island. We then called for volunteers to assist in the stoking of the ships and made all speed possible to Colombo; the whole convoy strung out, and went for it.

During the night, our main steam pipe burst and with difficulty we managed to reach Colombo by early morning. We anchored in the Colombo roadstead till the *Sydney* arrived, and orders were issued that the *Sydney* was not to be cheered as she entered the harbour with her dead. She had attacked and sunk the *Emden* off Kokos Island.

The next ship to enter the harbour was the *Empress of Russia*, an armed merchantman, with the German crew of the *Emden*. We were given leave in Colombo and I had the misfortune to miss the ship (It wasn't his fault for he had leave till 6 and the ship sailed at 4.) and I was forced to hire a steam pinnace and chase her out to sea. I picked up a crowd of men in the same position and took a collection from them. We succeeded in reaching her before she went too far. I got brought up before the captain, but he couldn't say much. We then sailed direct for Aden (Hell's Gate). We tried to enter before dawn and a shot was fired across our bows and we immediately turned about and stood out to sea again and did not go in again. We then proceeded to Suez. The ship was sandbagged round the decks because of the Turks and we were fired upon several times by rifles going through the canal. We coaled at Port Said. Leaving the harbour, French and British battleships were drawn up on either side. Both the French and British cheered us as we went through, and the British were very keen to know if we had any 'All Black' footballers aboard. Nothing serious happened on the voyage to Alexandria. I again became a soldier and went with the troops to Cairo.

We settled down in Cairo near Heliopolis, the garden suburb of Cairo. There is a big casino there, built by a Belgian firm, but they could not get a licence. Now a large hospital. It had taken us eight weeks to reach Alexandria and we got there about a week before Christmas.

We then settled down to heavy training. The first incident of note was that we had to man the streets of Cairo for the coronation of Hussein Kamel, Sultan of Egypt. The next was the big parade called for the purpose of declaring Egypt a British Protectorate.

During our stay in Heliopolis, I was in charge of a party who were digging pits for refuse and we came across the lost city of Heliopolis. We got to a tomb, moved the top slab and found skeletons. I then formed a party and we went excavating on our own without the permission of the Egyptian government. The houses and the tombs were intact inside, though the streets were silted up with sand. We tunnelled from 1 house to another and found several pieces of pottery and 1 ring. As there was such a large party of us, and not having an article apiece, we decided that we would sell our finds and divide the money between us.

We then went to the Suez Canal for its defence, January 3rd or 4th 1915, and on February 2nd took part in the battle against the Turks, when they were defeated. We only lost one man killed and one wounded, most of the fighting being done by Indian troops. We were in sand forts. There was only 1 white soldier to every 10 yards. Our brigade stretched from Suez to Port Said (about 5,000 men). We had then 1 brigade of infantry and 1 of mounted.

We left towards the end of February for the Dardanelles, travelling from Suez to Alexandria in open trucks (the peculiarity of the climate being intense heat of day which reached 110 and dropped to 50 or 60 during the night), most of the travelling being done during the night. We were then put onto transports and proceeded to Lemnos Island in the Grecian archipelago, where we found a large collection of French, British and Russian battleships, and close on 100 transports containing troops of all nationalities. Behind us, on the voyage, we towed a steam pinnace and 2 dhows. When we first got in touch with the islands of the archipelago, we ran into stormy weather. The pinnace and dhows broke loose and, as we had a Lascar crew aboard, the master of the ship called for volunteers from amongst the soldiers to assist in salvaging the pinnace and the dhows. The first mate and myself with 10 of our boys manned a lifeboat. We just managed to scramble out of the first lifeboat as she was smashed to pieces by a wave against the side of the ship. We manned a second lifeboat and managed to get clear. After rowing about for nearly 2 hours (in the big sea in the dark!) we salvaged and tried to get steam up in the pinnace, but found that she was in a sinking condition, and had to abandon her. We managed to get the dhows alongside the ship. The master of the ship made a bad move and brought the stern of the ship down on one of the dhows. The other dhow became entangled in the propeller and if it had not been for the presence of mind of Capt. McDonnell (an army captain) who ordered ropes to be thrown over the side, we would have lost our lives. We scrambled aboard up the ropes. I was in the dhow that got mixed up with the propeller.

Guy had dictated to me so far, when Bert Chesters came in from Blackheath and now I am afraid I shall never get the end of the story.

He was to have spent this Monday evening with us at Wanstead and on Saturday George brought down the news that he was to go into camp today (Monday) and would be sailing for New Zealand almost immediately. It is not at all likely that he will get a day up from camp, but he will if he can. I am very sorry and disappointed not to say goodbye to him, and feel quite sad at his going, though very glad to think of him getting home again. He has been with us so much, and has always been so willing and anxious to do anything and to help in any way, and so thoughtful. He is 28 so I did not feel the responsibility for him that I did for some of the boys. He was about a good deal with Mrs Herbert, his colonel's wife, who had come to England with her husband to run a canteen and look after the New Zealanders. She introduced him to numbers of nice girls – girls who lived in good clubs, many of them college girls. These girls gave 'at homes' and dances for the soldiers! It seems very funny to our ideas, but everything is so altered now, and there is so much more camaraderie than there was. At Christmas and in the New Year, Guy went to lots of dances, but he did not much enjoy them, for he does not know these new dances which are all the rage – the hesitation waltz, bunny hug, trots etc. When I was young it was thought improper to dance more than 3 dances with any man in an evening. Now it is usual to dance all the time with one man. Because the steps are so various, you have to know your partner's ways. (The first dance I went to when I was nearly 18, I did not know what was proper, and Mother had never been to a dance, and I danced 12 with one man, 8 with another, and the rest with a third, and the first two got annoyed with each other.)

Guy also has a wire round his ankle binding his sinews together, the result of some accident. He has had an extraordinary life. His mother died when he was a little boy, and he and his two younger brothers, the twins George and Will, were brought up by their father and housekeepers. Their father must be a harsh man, who had no sympathy with his boys. He used to send them to bed at 6 o'clock till Guy was well on in his teens and often pull them out of bed when he got home and thrash them. They did not know why, but Guy says there was sure to have been something he would have thrashed them for if he had known about it! They have a large house at Masterton and would often sit down 20 to dinner on a Sunday including maids and men who sat at the same table on Sundays. When he was 12 and his brothers 7, they went on a 3-month camping expedition by themselves. He did splendidly at college on the mathematical side and then his father insisted on his coming into his business to which he greatly objected and he was evidently a demon in the workshops.

He left his father, and we have heard bits of the next 5 years of his life. He was a professional runner, and for the year he ran made £300 besides expenses. But he gave it up because it was not true sport. Men would be bribed not to do their best. He was gold digging and sifting in the South Island, at first with a very rich uncle whose books he kept, and then on his own. He said it was extraordinary what men you met in the gold fields. One day a man had his leg smashed. Guy was going off in a car for a doctor – 40 miles – when another man said, 'I can fix this up. I am fully qualified surgeon,' and he did. He went opal getting in Queensland, and got 1 gorgeous opal which he sold for £30 because he was hard up. He says he is going to get me an opal if he can (but I think he can't). In Sydney he was once so hard up that he had not a penny. He became ships' engineer and knows, and has worked on, practically all the boats round New Zealand.

When he came to us first he said he had not slept in a proper bed for 7 years. The first notion he got that his father loved him was when he saw his eyes full of tears as he said goodbye to his 3 boys to go to the war. And yet he seemed quite to like quiet evenings with George and me and was so nice about the house. I should think he has no fear.

When the *Penguin* went down at Wellington, volunteers were called for to go to her. He was one. The weather was awful, and for hours they could not get to her, and were in very great danger themselves. Then there was the story of the dhows when he was a volunteer. He told us one day how he had climbed out along a great crane at the top of a building in Farringdon Street to set something right, and the people shrieked to him to go back.

He is very clever with engineering and in all sorts of practical ways. He mended lots of things for us – fenders, lampshades etc. and made me 3 lampshades.

He has the 'Meritorious Service' Cross about which he is very shy, and we have heard very little about why he had it, but he acknowledged that a lot of Generals came down to see him. At some very critical time, I think in 1916, after a great battle, he went out with his men over the field and collected guns and parts of them and renovated them and supplied over 300 to New Zealand and British divisions. In the disaster last April, he was mixed up in the retreat. He was behind the lines with his 'shop', and was suddenly told to pack up and be off in a very short time and report at a certain place. He started off with his 7 lorries piled up and wandered about, sometimes actually mixed up with Germans, for the town he was to report at was occupied by Germans when he got there, and sometimes he found himself going parallel with German lines. He could find no headquarters for directions where to go, but at last he got his lorries into safety, only losing 1 which had broken down.

When he came to England, he was very much knocked up and that was why he was sent here. He had been out since the beginning of the war – he had a terrible time in Gallipoli. He was 1 of 8 remaining out of 600 and was so weak and ill he had to be taken to hospital and then went direct to France. After he returned from camp at Sling (Bulford), he worked at the New Zealand arms depot in Farringdon Road. He is armourer sergeant, and would not take a commission. He, and all the boys who come to us, are so careful about their personal appearance.

One night, Ivy Newton and Mr Boyce, a lieutenant to whom she is engaged and who has been wounded in the arm and had 16 operations on it, were here to dinner, and Guy came. I thought he looked very strange, and very white. The next time I saw him, I asked him if he was ill, and he said he had been to the barber's and he had forgotten that he had powdered his face! These wretched barbers make no end out of the boys. They charge them outrageous prices, and get them to buy all sorts of things. Anything from 10/- they will get. Bert the other day thought 6/- quite cheap to get out with paying. The shops in the Strand charge the men for clothing, just in the same ratio.

Guy told us an interesting detail about General Birdwood and General Godly respectively. General Birdwood at Gallipoli walked about dressed as his men, without a staff, talking with them and cheering them even in the very front trenches. He slept on a ledge cut out of the rock. General Godly walked about at the back of the lines, fully dressed, accompanied always by his staff, and when the lines were so thin the men could hardly be relieved, employed about 1,000 digging him a huge dugout.

Lady Godly ran a hospital or something of that kind on Lemnos Island (I think) and any boy she took a fancy to got promoted. The consequence was that General Godly was hated, General Birdwood is adored.

Christmas 1918. We had a very happy Christmas – the first 'Peace' Christmas. I had dreaded it, the first one without dear Father and Mother, but it was much happier than I expected.

Guy arrived on Monday to stay till Saturday, and in the evening took down a turkey to Mr Waights for us, and the next morning helped me round with a lot of presents. Rod Piper came to lunch and I asked Margaret Bedells in too. He told us something of his terrible experiences in Germany, but not much. He got neuritis very badly, and could not walk, but the Germans pretended he was malingering and would kick him when he fell. Then he was put in prison and was very ill, and I think the Armistice only just saved him. He was in prison in Belgium, and the guards took the men out, took them a little way, the train broke down, and they left them. Some Belgians were very good to Rod and after getting along some distance he was picked up by an English lorry, I think, and taken to hospital and then sent on to hospital here. He was much better when he came to lunch, but could not walk far. He was with friends for Christmas. We had asked Mr McCrae up, and he said he would come if he could. He was in camp and expecting to go home any day. He did not come, and we have not heard from him again so perhaps he has gone.

Maud and Harold arrived in the afternoon. I had not seen them since October. Christmas Day we all went to chapel (it was the first time Guy had been to church for years) and in the afternoon Mrs Haigh and her 2 daughters came in for a few minutes and Mr de Moulpied. We had sent him a turkey and he had 4 sailors for dinner.

In the evening Miss Hall, Will and Mary, Mrs Forster and Courtney came to dinner. We had soup, a large boiled turkey which George had had great difficulty in getting, a Xmas pudding made more than 2 years ago, which was <u>delicious,</u> little cheese savouries made with New Zealand cheese and sweets which I had been collecting for weeks. You can only buy a few at a time, and I had sent a lot out to different boys in France and in camp. We had another pudding in reserve in case the old one was not nice, made of fruit which Guy had brought us, but sultanas had been impossible to get and he could not get much peel. We had managed to make a little mincemeat, having got 1 lb of apples a few days before Christmas. We played games after dinner.

Harold and Maud stayed till Saturday. We played auction bridge in the evenings. Guy is teaching me and I am sure it must have been very dull for him to do that, but they would not let me ask someone else in, and me sit out. Neither would they go to a theatre because of leaving me at home. It was very sweet of them, but I was sorry about it. On Saturday after H. and M. had gone, George, Guy and I went to Will and Mary's for dinner and G. and I stayed on till Tuesday.

Guy spent the first Sunday in the New Year with us, and we went to a very interesting service at St. John's church in the afternoon, a united service. Mr Ream preached from the pulpit, the vicar conducted the service. Dr Ramsey, Presbyterian, prayed, and also the Baptist minister, and other clergy and ministers were present. The following Sunday, the Vicar of St. Peter's preached from our pulpit. These two services marked the beginning and end of a week of united prayer, and a clergyman had never preached from Archway Road pulpit, nor a Wesleyan from the church pulpit. It is an effort to show the 'man in the street' that we are not divided in principle, and shows that the idea of 'union' is gradually penetrating, and that we are beginning to understand each other better.

When we got home from the afternoon service we found a telephone message to say that Bert Chesters had rung up and would be out about 4.30. He arrived, not looking at all well. He had had 3 days and nights in a cattle truck, with only very hard biscuits and marmalade to eat, not even a hot drink anywhere. They could not lie down, they were too tightly packed, and even had to stand part of the time. Bert had got in on Saturday evening, and had been 3 hours tramping to try to find a bed for the night. He would not come straight out to us because of a certain reason. Part of his furlough he spent with relations at Liverpool, the next with us and at Ethel's. He took Joyce to a matinee, and very much liked talking about 'a little English girl'. He says he could listen to English girls talking all day. Their pronunciation is so different to the Australian girls and they talk with a hesitation. Bernard helped him to arrange with 'Liptons' to go there for 2 months and he hoped to get demobilised in England, but missed the demobilisation officer. He went to Cambridge for the day on Saturday, but only had 2 hours there as he wanted to see this man then the train was so late that he missed him. It took over 4 hours to get from Cambridge to King's Cross. That is the way with our trains now. The services are shocking. To Blackheath there is 1 train an hour!

We had a little party. Bert, Guy, Joyce, Dorothy Morton, Alison Carr, Margaret Biddles.

Bert went off before 6.00 on Monday morning, in good spirits with hopes of soon being back again.

Gerard and his fiancée came to dinner on Monday and stayed the night. They are to be married on February 12th.

February 4th. I was to have gone to Wanstead on the Tuesday but had a sore throat so did not come till the Saturday. I thought I should clear all the boys and Guy was coming to spend evenings here, but on the Monday

Guy rang up to say he had just heard that he was to go to camp that very day to sail for New Zealand the end of the week. I was very sad not to say goodbye to him, but he managed to get up to town again on Tuesday and on Wednesday came here to say goodbye. It was nice of him. I felt saying goodbye very much. He has been so nice about the house, and is a most clever man. He felt saying goodbye to us too, and told George he could never say what our home had meant to him. He was going back to Sling that night, and would be up at 5 o'clock in the morning superintending the loading of trains for the boat at Tilbury. Then he would probably travel down on a goods train to Tilbury on Thursday night. He was going to try to get over again on Friday, but did not come and we have not heard from him, so I suppose his boat SS *Hororata* sailed on Saturday. He said he should be very busy all the voyage out demobilising the men. He had 4 clerks with him. He talks of coming back again to bring over more men. 8 of them are to return, but I think probably he will find he is wanted at Masterton when he gets there.

There are 5 of our boys now on the sea. Gainor and Clarence Lane who sailed for New Zealand just before Christmas (we had letters from them last week. Gainor's from Colombo, Clarence Lane's from Colón, Panama); Frank Brown, who sailed Monday in last week also for New Zealand; Murray Sinclair [on] Wednesday for Sydney; and Guy on Saturday.

Last Friday Jim turned up. I had been awfully worried about him, not having heard anything for a month, and he always wrote every week. Finally, George enquired at Horseferry Road. I was afraid he might have had an accident in Paris. It turns out that 2 letters have not reached us. He had had the same experience as Bert. George and I were both at Wanstead but Alice put him to bed with hot water bottles and bread and milk, and George brought him down here on Saturday and Sunday to see me. He came in one evening. He could not speak, he was so bad. Bert says the Belgians cannot do enough for the soldiers. They are all eager to take them into their homes and make much of them. Bert is at a Boulanger and when he first went into his bedroom there were only candles. The next night electric light had been fixed. Madame made him slippers when she found his shoes hurt him, and her little daughter calls him 'mon cher Albert'.

February 6th. George and Jim came to Wanstead on Tuesday and Jim recited. George had a rough throat and when he came down on Wednesday about 4.30, in deep snow, he had hardly any voice. I was very worried, partly lest it might be a cold and the cousins might catch it, partly lest he should be ill there. Also, because of the miners' strike, the coal ration has been greatly reduced, only temporarily we hope. The cousins should have 13½ tons a year, and they have been told they can only have half a ton a month, not more than enough for the kitchen fire! It is very hard at their age – Mary over 80, Jessie nearly 80 and so delicate, and I don't know what is to be done. They did not think the coal would last longer than Saturday. They had ordered it long ago and it had not come. They unfortunately deal with Warren's as we do, about the worst firm possible at the present time.

These strikes are abominable. It was what was predicted after the war. The tube men have struck for a 40-hour week. This was promised, and now they want luncheon time out of it. What decent man should want to work only 6 hours a day? There is this dreadful strike going on in Scotland, and this evening the electricians said they should strike and leave London in darkness and a lot of machinery would be affected too. However, the Government said that a fine of £100 or 6 months' imprisonment would be inflicted on each man who struck, also that they had made arrangements for carrying on the lighting, and the lights have not gone out this evening yet. We heard at Wanstead this morning that the millers had struck, and that the Wanstead bakers had only flour for two days so, considering the coal and that the cousins burnt more when we were there, and the bread, and George's throat we decided to come home.

The weather was so awful and I had not been out since my arrival, that we decided to have a motor home. The man charged 30/-, but it was well worth it, though we were home in half an hour! Doris was coming on

Saturday, but I have put her off at any rate till Monday, as one does not know what is going to happen with all these strikes.

February 28th. The cousins got coal in the day after we left, but no one is allowed to have more than half a ton a month, and with the very cold weather we have had for so long we must burn more than that. We cannot get logs, but fortunately there are still some from the garden and we use coke, but that comes in our coal allowance. It has been very difficult to get oil, too, and what we have been able to get is of poor quality. We never have more than 1 fire a day upstairs. Food conditions are improving. We can get apples now, and though we have to give up our coupons at the butcher's still, we can get practically as much meat as we want. Margarine is to be uncouponed on March 2nd. Lard is already uncouponed, but everything is still very dear. George brought home tonight peppermint creams, and walnut toffee. It must be years since they have been for sale.

Doris arrived on the Monday, and she made Jim's holiday much livelier for him. He spent it all here – 17 days, for he took 3 days extra, and he wrote to me that he had enjoyed every minute of it. We had some people in and he and Doris and I went to two theatres, the Court to see *Twelfth Night*, and the Savoy to see *Nothing but the Truth*. He was very lively and recited a great deal splendidly and was very nonsensical. He is a darling.

He left at 5 o'clock in the morning of a Monday and had a better journey back as he arrived at his village on Thursday, and spent a day and night of that time at a rest camp in Calais.

On the night he left, last Monday week, we had Bay Piper here for the night – a very nice great big fellow. He thanked us so for letting him come! And said it was only the third time he had been in a home since he left Australia in 1914. He was with us for dinner once last summer. We would gladly have seen more of him. He told me of his 'love' in Australia and bought a bag for her at Liberty's. He sailed last Tuesday, leaving camp at 4 o'clock on Sunday morning. We also had a letter from Mr McCrae saying he was leaving Thursday in last week. We can't think what has happened to Bert. He wrote that he was leaving France with a draft for Australia, via England, last Monday 3 weeks, and we have been expecting him ever since, and have heard nothing. Letters have come for him and a parcel.

Last Monday, February 24th, Harry Brooker was here for the night, in great spirits as he is expecting to be married in less than 3 weeks, and he is very much in love with his Betty. He is in an English regiment, and has not been demobilised yet.

Influenza has assumed an epidemic form again. In Manchester and Liverpool schools and theatres are closed. On Monday, Alice left hurriedly to go to her sister, who had pneumonia, following influenza. She is getting better happily, but in trying to get a woman to help with the work here, I found that influenza is everywhere, and every woman who had not got it herself is nursing it. The minister at Finchley has died, and everyone in his house was down with it. Poor little Mrs Keane told me that her mother had had it, and could not even get a woman in to help, and then her sister had taken ill with pneumonia, and the doctor could not get a nurse anywhere, and she had to be taken to the infirmary [she died]. It is impossible to get maids or women. The James McDonalds have had no one for months. Funerals are continually passing, and there are 'influenza queues' at the surgeries. It is so very difficult to get the people buried. We read in the papers that business is at a standstill in Australia because of it – even the banks being closed, and in Auckland in New Zealand on Armistice Day there were so many ill that rejoicing could not be held, and the bells were not rung on account of the many sick. In South Africa it was the same, all business closed, and the people who were well taking food to the people who were ill. Emma nearly died, 1 of her maids did die, and Alfred had to do the nursing. The papers are full of deaths – 'pneumonia following influenza'. There is no doubt, I think, that it is some sort of a plague, and not flu, and probably arising from the unsanitary conditions on the Continent. So many dead, and so many men herded together.

Yesterday and today the furniture and household goods were sold at Brathay, and things have sold wonderfully well – war prices. About £900 has been realised, Harold says.

April 4th. On March 4th, Bert Chesters rang up to say he was in England. The bachelors' room was being spring cleaned, and the spare room was full of rubbish that I was sorting, but Alice was very nice, and we soon cleared the spare room for him. He has joined the Australian 'Educational' whatever you call it, and has gone to Liptons for 2 months. He stayed with us for a fortnight. He would not have stayed quite so long but he could not get reasonable rooms. He could get nothing decent under £2.10.0 a week, and I asked Mrs Parker if they knew of anyone who would take him, and they most kindly took him themselves for 35/- a week, so he is very comfortably settled, and is also getting on well at Liptons learning the tea trade. He was served out a 'civvie' suit, but it was no fit!

George and Will Wagg have both been up to see us. Will has the Military Medal. He won it at the Forêt de Memel. The New Zealanders, in the great advance last October, had been held up trying to get round the forest, so at last they went through it. It was like a German fort, and when they came to the other side the men were demoralised and he rallied them. He is a most cheerful, casual soul. He said he never thought he would be killed. Practically the only time he really felt miserable was when he was wounded in the shoulder. He was bandaged up and had to walk for 6 hours before he got anywhere where he could get help. Most of the time he was alone, and could only direct himself in the dark by going towards the glare of our big guns. He was in hospital 2 months, but did not get to 'Blighty', and his people thought he had only a scratch.

So many of these boys are rheumatic after all the exposure they have had. I fear it may tell upon their constitutions in years to come.

On March 18th, a Tuesday, I had a wire from Harry Brooker from Dover asking if he could come up for the night. When he arrived I said, 'Well, Harry, and when is the wedding to be?' and he said, 'On Thursday, and, Mrs Scales, may I bring Betty straight back here?' My breath was nearly taken away, but I managed to say, 'We shall be delighted if you will,' but how we have laughed about it. I said that if Betty would rather not come, I should quite understand! However, they duly arrived on Thursday evening, and we had white flowers on the table and the silver table centre, and a little silver shoe with orange blossom in it. We made ourselves as scarce as possible during the honeymoon, which only lasted till the Monday – short enough – poor young things. They had a fire and themselves (in spite of coal shortage!) and went everywhere, even to church, alone. Betty was the sweetest, prettiest little thing, and reminded me so much of Joyce. Harry wired to ask for extension of leave, and on Sunday came back the curt wire 'No'. The army is horrid. In a letter which he wrote to us, he said, 'My thoughts continually go back to the few days we spent at Elm Bank. They were such strenuous days – but I shall not forget them for to me they were perfect happiness.' He <u>was</u> so delighted that we liked Betty and thought her so sweet. It was 'quite pathetic', and when I spoke of moving from here, he seemed quite upset, and said he did hope we should not, as he felt this house was his 'standby'.

The papers are full just now of the use of aeroplanes for commerce, mails, and travel. They flew to Paris the other day in 1 hour 40 minutes, and it is said that aeroplanes will get to Australia in 5 days. I had a very amusing letter from little Margaret in Adelaide. She said, 'Would you ever dream of coming out here in the airoplain that takes 5 days to get here? It would be quite easy because you would just pack up a nightgown and a brush and comb and a diomand necklace and other necessary things and get on. Then when you got this end you would get off and meat me going to my music lesson, but of course you would bring Uncle George with you?' I wonder if I shall ever go in one. George would like to.

The great triple alliance strike – miners, railway men and transport workers – has been averted for the present, but everything seems in a terribly unsettled condition. This unemployment pay, which the Government is giving now to 1 million people, is demoralising and abominable.

1 of the clerks at the office, to whom they have been giving half pay during his time in the army, and for whom, at his request, they applied for to get him demobilised more quickly, after he had been back at the office a week, gave notice, left and today enquiries have come from the 'unemployment bureau'. He just wants to get a holiday, and payment for doing nothing. The girls will not go into service, and now they are being given half pay – 15/- a week – until October. The Government is mad. All trades are in a ferment because of the way Government is interfering with them. The Chambers of Commerce and the merchants and shippers etc. are continually having indignation meetings but it does no good. George was at a great luncheon the other day at which Runceman spoke and the chairman gave two instances of Government interference and chicanery which George had given him – McDonald Scales were shipping some machinery to the South Australian Government, when just as it was going, the AG telephoned asking them to transfer the shipping to them as thereby they would save 70% in freight.

The second was, 18 months ago McD. S. & Co. had all their rabbits commandeered by the Government, who, however, refused to pay for them or to ship them. The FOB price Sydney was 19/- a crate and they asked them last year to buy them back at 45/- delivered London. They had been in cold storage more than a year, and were also skinned – not in their fur, as they might have been. When they refused to do such a mad thing, they said, 'Very well, we shall not let you have any freight for your new season's lot till ours are cleared out of the way.' But I could go on giving similar instances. Herbert Newton had a tremendous affair with the Government and only at last got the money owing to him from them – £10,000 – by threatening to go to law and make the whole transaction public.

Our choir men are coming back again and it is so nice to see men everywhere again – on trains, trams etc. There is no doubt that in all trades there has been tremendous profiteering. All drapery goods were most frightfully dear this year, and now that the company reports are coming out – Harrods, Swan & Edgar's etc. – they all report a year of unprecedented profit! You can't get a decent coat and skirt under £10, and to get now what we used to get for about £7, you now have to pay £15. 'Cheap' hats are £3.3.0! I did not get a warm coat last winter, because I could not get even a cloth for less than £13.13.0, and that was hideous – very clumsy and ordinary.

Harry told us the other night how he got his wound. Through faulty information to headquarters he was sent with two men right behind the German lines, and found himself within a few feet of rear German lines. They opened fire at close range, and he was shot through the arm (and in the thigh?). His men ran away, and bullets or shrapnel peppered all round him and even under his legs which were drawn up, but nothing more hit him, and he lay all night not daring to move lest the Germans should fire at him again. It was a November night, and he was lying a pool of water, feeling his blood flowing. It was a wonder that he lived. In the morning the Germans, finding he was still living, took him into hospital.

July 10th. It is a long time since I have written in this book, but now that Peace has been declared, I must finish it.

Peace was declared on Saturday, June 28th. Some people thought that the Germans would not sign, that it would be impossible for them to accept the terms, but they had been brought so low that I felt sure they must. But as they signed under protest, and simply because of *force majeure* one feels that they would regard this treaty as 'a scrap of paper' if they could, and everyone (of any sense) is sure that they will only keep it by the rest of the world making it impossible for them to break it. One hopes that, in time, a better spirit will grow up in Germany but a great change will have to come over them. One hopes too that a Labour government which will undo by politics all that has been gained in the war with so much pain and hardship will not come in to power.

A general distrust of Germany made it impossible to rejoice greatly. On that Saturday, Ridley Reed rang up asking if he could come to lunch to say goodbye as he was going into camp on Monday. He had been to see us in March. He is a very energetic man, 23 years old, and 1 of Arthur's postulants. On the way to the war, he had prepared about 70 in the ship for confirmation and as he had come to France through Italy he bought an 'ikon' in Italy which he had carried about with him. He was a gunner or driver. He bought all sorts of things in England for his study – images of a 'sarcophagus' and asked us for 1 of our figures of a monk. He wishes to have a very special atmosphere in his study and is not going to allow smoking in it. He is also dead against marriage and intends to be a celibate, and devote his rectory to the parish, making a sort of home of it. He is quite a character and I wonder what his future will be.

He left about 5.30, just as Harry and Betty arrived. They were to sail on Monday, and came up from Swaffham Prior for the night. They had already been to Devonport a fortnight before. Poor little Betty parted from all her people, and they got here on Saturday night about 10 o'clock having been much delayed on journey and travelling in the guard's van. Her sister came to tea with them on Sunday, and on Monday we said a rather sad goodbye. On Tuesday we expected a card to say they were off, but nothing came, and on Friday we had a letter to say they were back at Swaffham Prior. When they got to Devonport, they found a confusion of passengers, babies, luggage and no boat. The army headquarters at Winchester had actually known there would be no boat. It was detained in Liverpool by a strike, but they allowed all these poor people to go right down to Devonport (7 hours' railway journey from London) to 'report'! They then gave them tickets to return home, but numbers of people would have nowhere to return to, having made their arrangements up to the last minute, and houses or lodgings are almost impossible to get now.

They left us finally on Sunday, June 29th, and no doubt are well on their way now. [Their engines broke down, and they were delayed a further 10 days at Plymouth.]

George was very much inclined to go up to London in the evening to try to see something of the Peace demonstrations. We had heard the old familiar sound of the guns at 6 o'clock in the afternoon reminding us of many air raids. How glad we should have been in 1916–17–18 to know for certain that one day we should hear those same guns firing as the signal of the 'Peace'. However, Harry had a headache and I was not very keen, so he did not go. The next day we heard from Mr Willis that he and his wife had been through London on a bus and had seen the great but very orderly crowds, and the only excitement had been that an old lady on the top of the bus had got set on fire by a cracker. We had an impromptu Thanksgiving service on Sunday, for no special service was ready! George had made several enquiries for one, but they said it could not be printed as the date was not known! People are queer. George, however, found some very nice prayers, and he had to take part of the service himself.

We also got up early in the morning to hang out flags, and our house was the gayest in the neighbourhood. We strung flags of the British Empire and the Allies right across the garden, and had 5 standards in 5 tubs and large flags out of the top windows, and over the front door. How I wish my dear Father and Mother had lived to see Peace declared. I am sure the war was responsible for Father's depression. The horror and strangeness of it weighed very heavily on him, and I think caused his illness. People simply cannot be gay for I should think everyone has lost those they love. But one can be, and is, thankful.

Everything is still very unsettled in domestic affairs. Food is just as dear as ever. Strawberries 1/6–2/- a lb. Currants 1/3. Raspberries 1/6–2/-. All groceries <u>at least</u> doubled. Bacon 2/6. Butter 2/6. Meat 2/-. Veal 3/-. Fish for a short time was cheaper, but what was uncontrolled very soon went up again. Cod, sold in the market at 6*d*, was 1/2 the very cheapest in the shops. Clothes are more expensive than ever. Cheapest Axminster stair carpet 16/- a yard. Vegetables awful. But you can get things if you pay the price. It is said that coal will be scarcer than last year and 6/- a ton dearer. I would rather have food short than coal. Wood is as dear as it was last winter. The profiteering is shocking. Train fares have 50% put on their proper price. Laundry the same, besides every article having the price higher as well. Our income tax is 6/8 in the pound. Our gardener is now asking 10/- a day. We give him 9/-.

We wanted to have had our house done up, but labour, paints and everything are so very dear. Also we have thought that we might move. People are curiously restless and unsettled, no doubt a result of the nerve strain everyone has been through. However, we have now decided to remain where we are, but we shall have to spend a lot on our house, as during the war, for patriotic reasons, we let everything that we could stand over to be done till the war was over. But it would have been better for our pockets to have done it up while the war was on! It is almost impossible to get moderate-sized houses and numbers of people who have sold theirs can get nothing, and are homeless. Hotels and boarding houses are consequently crowded, and houses are selling at high prices. In spite of this difficulty about houses, we had no offer for ours, because it was a half basement! Maids are difficult to get, because the government is still giving this unemployment money.

July 18th. I am writing this in bed at 10.30 at night, and guns are firing and one thinks of those dreadful nights not so very long ago, but the firing now is the beginning of the Peace rejoicings, and tomorrow is the great day of rejoicing which we used often to think of and wonder if it would ever come. It is wonderful to think that it has really come, and that what our heroes died for has come to pass. But it will be a sad day for many whose dear ones lie in the fields of France, Belgium and in Gallipoli and the Far East. George has not wanted to go to see either the procession or the illuminations, so we are having a quiet day at home and the maids are going out. Bernard and Ethel and Honor are going to a stand in Westminster Road and only have to pay £2.2.0 each for the seats. They wanted us to go with them and we were also invited to the Home Office and to Hyde Park Hotel for the illuminations at night. I think it is very slow and dull to do nothing, but it is what George wishes. He was at Whitehall today and said the streets were packed, people even sitting all along the kerbs. I saw some of the city decorations: Mansion House and Bank, and round there, and the decorations up west must be lovely.

September 4th. We had it fine on July 19th until about 3 o'clock, but it was lovely for the procession. Then a drizzle came on, and it drizzled more or less all the evening, which must have spoilt a great many fireworks. We saw the great flares round London. There was one on Shepherd's Hill, and a number of private people had fireworks as well as the great display in Hyde Park.

I will tell, now, Reg Dunn's story, for he was the first of our boys to come and he is the last to go. On August 1st of last year [1918] he came home on leave. We were going to Amersham the next day, so he came down to us there, stayed a night, then went on to Ethel for 2 or 3 nights, and then to Llandudno by himself from Wednesday to Saturday. On Saturday morning, the telephone went and Reg's voice, 'Well, Mrs Scales, I've something to tell you. I'm in love,' and he had met a girl haphazard on the parade at Llandudno and taken her out in a boat, where the tide or current nearly swept them out to sea. She showed Reg that she was 'fond of him' (!) and he went head over heels. Bern and Ethel, George and I, all talked very plainly to him. Ways between girls and soldiers are very free and easy now, but no girl of his class would have acted or allowed him to act as she did. He was most open and sweet about it, and did not mind anything we said, and I much hoped that the year in France would make the impression wear off. However, they corresponded and when he came home in May he came straight to Wanstead where I was staying, and said he was going up to Leicester, and if he still felt the same when he saw Eve, might he bring her to us. Of course, he is a man – he is 23 – and we had no power to interfere, so I said yes, and in a few days he brought her, and she was very much what I expected. She has lovely hair and complexion and is a pretty girl and dresses nicely and sings well, but no class. He is desperately in love, but she, I think, not so much. We had the brother and his wife over. Mr and Mrs Arthur Rich, pleasant people with sensible ideas, but common.

Reg and she had a most tragic farewell when Reg went back to camp, and I was grieved for them both. However, it has proved not by any means to be the last goodbye, for he was sent to camp and got various 'leaves' and in

July was taken very ill when in Leicester, her home. He did not go straight into hospital, as his boat was to sail on the 23rd, and he was afraid of being reported sick. However, one night he lost 3 pints of blood from his throat and the doctor sent him into hospital. From there he was sent to Dartford. He was then put on the boat roll of a hospital ship, sailing August 26th, and through a clerical error he, and 7 others, were left off that. He came through London to go back to camp the same day and came here, but we were away, and the poor boy was dreadfully upset by it all.

Last night at 9 o'clock he rang up from Fenchurch Street to say he was actually on his way to his boat, the *Karanga* and he came out for the night, and left at 8 this morning. The boat sails on September 8th, and he hoped to get leave to go to Leicester tonight, but though it sounds cruel, I hope he won't, lest something more should happen! He was in Leicester 10 days ago. I have said goodbye 4 times to him. The first one he was very much upset, poor boy, because of parting with Eve too. The second he gave me a great hug on Crouch End platform. The third was sad too, but this last one we could only laugh.

Reg is very anxious to get Eve into different surroundings and Mrs Alice Dorey has very kindly offered that she should go to her for 3 months and she and Miss Gregory will train her in household duties and cooking so that she can take a better sort of position.

September 6th. It was really goodbye to Reg yesterday morning, for in the evening he rang up from North Woolwich. He was on his boat, they had been unloading and arranging the medical stores all day. They were to sail for Devonport today, and no leave allowed. The poor old boy was very disappointed not to go to Leicester again, and I wonder when I shall hear his voice again! He sailed on the *Karanga* [Shaw Saville, carrying 850 men].

We had by the post this morning letters from Harry and Betty Brooker, from Cape Town, dated August. They had been delayed 10 days at Plymouth, several days on the voyage, and a further 10 days at Cape Town, by engine trouble. We also had a letter from Jim posted in Adelaide July 16th, so his journey has been safe so far. We said goodbye to him on April 24th and George April 26th when he went back to camp. He left for Australia end of April so he has been a long time on the way. I had a letter of 30 pages from him from Cape Town and I think he will be the one of all the boys whom we are likely to keep in closest touch with, and he was the one we loved most. I was very fond of Jack Dunn, but he has only written once, or perhaps twice since he went home, which is rather disappointing. Guy Wagg has only written once, but I did not expect him to write, for he can't. He is such a clever man, but he cannot spell. He once signed a letter to me 'Yours truelly'.

Jim came home from France on April 11th, and when we went to Milford with Ethel and Bern, he went to

Scotland and then joined us at Milford. He was with us from Saturday to Thursday, I think, and he said he had never enjoyed a holiday so much in his life. It was good of Eth and Bern to have him. On Easter Sunday, he went to church with us morning and evening. We had a lovely drive in the New Forest, and Ethel, he, I, Honor and Joyce spent a day in the Isle of Wight. We had most delightful rooms at Milford on the cliff 'Mentay'. We did feel saying goodbye to him, and he to us. He had 2 days with George at Elm Bank before going to camp. I had a letter from him every day before he left England.

Bert Chesters left Mrs Parkins on June 21st and came to us for a few days. Then, with some difficulty, for he cannot make up his mind, I got him off to Scotland and he enjoyed himself so much there that he did not come back for more than a fortnight. We said goodbye to him on July 15th when he and Ridley Reed, who had been staying a night, went to camp together. He was a dear, kind boy, but George could never hear what he said, he spoke so softly, so he used rather to annoy George and I used to be always saying, 'Speak up.' He would not go anywhere by himself. On Sunday evening, August 22nd, he rang up from town saying he was on his way to join his boat, the *Kinowna*. She ought to have gone 3 weeks earlier, but kept being put off. She sailed from Southampton on August 26th, and I had a very nice letter from him from the ship.

We had a letter from Murray Sinclair last week saying that he was safely back and in his father's office, going to be married. We also had a letter from Silas Wright a little while ago saying that he was to be married this month.

Marland Nield was here on June 8th and we have not heard if he got off, but I think he must have gone, and gone suddenly, or he would have written. He is the only 1 of the boys we have not heard from. Mr McCrae got home after great difficulty. He had been hanging about in camp for ages. Gainor Jackson lost his mother about 3 months after he got home, so that poor boy lost father, mother and his 2 elder brothers in 13 months. Also, his father's trustees had behaved badly about the business and seem to have got it for themselves.

Peace having been signed, and the last of our Colonials having now sailed for their homes, and our special piece of war work being finished, I now conclude this very incomplete and sketchy record. As I have not been well enough to do outside work, both George and I felt we should use our house for people who needed help.

Lillie Scales, Elm Bank, Hornsey Lane.

October, 1919.

We have entertained for long or short periods:

Madame and Mademoiselle Gervais, Antwerp
Monsieur and Madame Massey and Raymond Massey, Brussels
Millicent Berry, Melbourne
Mrs Alban Jackson

Colonials
Serg. Dallas Taylor, New Zealand
Reginald, Jack and Cecil Dunn, Adelaide, South Australia
Guy, Will and George Wagg, Masterton, New Zealand
Ernest, Alban and Gainor Jackson, Auckland, New Zealand
Frank Brown, Te Kopura, New Zealand
Silas Wright, New Brunswick, Canada
G. S. H. McKay, Canterbury, New Zealand
Walter Bradley, Sydney, New South Wales
Amess B. Coleman, Sydney, New South Wales
Bay and Rod Piper, Adelaide, South Australia
Harry Brooker and Betty Brooker, Adelaide, South Australia
Arthur Brooker, Adelaide, South Australia
Bert Chesters, Ipswich, Queensland
Jim Gibb, Sydney, New South Wales
Murray Sinclair, Sydney, New South Wales
Marland Nield, Sydney, New South Wales
Alexander McCrae, Perth, Western Australia
A. C. Stephens, Dunedin, New Zealand
Clarence Lane, Totara North, New Zealand
A. J. Kendall Baker, Adelaide, South Australia
H. Rupert Brown, Fullarton, South Australia
Alan E. Black, Sydney, New South Wales
Ridley Reid, Alberton, South Australia
D. G. Moore, Claremont, South Australia
Eric Marshall, Adelaide, New South Wales

Pal O' Mine

When a chap is feeling lonely, and
  he's far from home and friends.
Happy then he counts the blessings as
  the breath of God descends
To bring him a comrade, staunch
  and loyal, brave and true
A Friend to love and cherish, a pal,
  and brother too
One to make the task grow lighter, one
  to make life more bright,
Whose 'heart and soul' whose every
  smile reflects a godly light;
One of truth, and love, and honour,
  living Christ-like every day
    Pal O' Mine

Like a summer breeze from heaven,
  floating o'er the ocean tide,
When the sea is sad and listless, you

were wafted by my side.
Like the song of birds in springtime,
   like the smile of sun at dawn,
A lonely heart grew brighter,
   a comradeship was born.
Then sorrows were as nothing, the
   skies were always blue,
The song was light, the path was
   bright, when shared along with you
The spirit that envoked us both to
   come and play our part,
Was the spirit that responded in a call
   from heart to heart.
     Pal O' Mine

In foreign climes, one summer-time, our
   brotherhood began,
And I could see (so happily) God's
   image in a man,
In Belgian town, French dale and
   down, on Egypt's sandy plain,
We prayed for loved ones back at
   home, and to return again.
But God decreed for (heaven did need
   in her celestial land)
Another soul of love and truth, to
   grace her saintly band.
So now I pray to Christ each day, as

oft I think of thee,
To help me be to those on earth, what
thou has been to me,
Pal O' Mine

In loving memory of my old pal Roy Bice, MM
Killed in Action, October 29th, 1917

J. T. Gibb, 7th Field Ambulance,
6 November 1917

Comparative Figures of Australian and Canadian Forces

The former has suffered more both absolutely and relatively with its population of 5,000,000 than has Canada with its population of 8,000,000.

Australia		Canada	
Total casualties	289,723	Total casualties	211,057
Deaths	57,000	Deaths	50,234
Wounded	229,123	Wounded	152,779
Prisoners and Missing	3,400	Prisoners and Missing	8,245
Total enlistments	417,000		
Embarked for overseas	330,000		

Letter from Reginald Dunn to Lillie, March 1949

My Dear English Folk

... we are so glad that Wendy Gibb was with you for Christmas. I do not know her but well remember her father Jim. Events do synchronise at times. Fancy Jim's daughter going to England to eat our cake which we sent you at your home where we ate so much of your cake and, incidentally, must have arrived at times when it was most inconvenient or tiresome for you.

But, being English, you would never give us the slightest clue that our frequent visits in any way contravened your week's programme.

How tired Mr Scales must have been on returning from a difficult day of business sometimes, only to discover on returning to his haven of refuge that a Dunn or a Chester or a Gibb was again in possession of his Englishman's Castle!

Our love to you both, R. H. S. Dunn.

Also available from Amberley Publishing

Tommies Recount Their WWI Trench Experiences

'Full of humour and laughter in the face of adversity' *BRITISH ASSOCIATION FOR LOCAL HISTORY*

Shortly after the end of the First World War, the most popular London newspaper of the time, *The Evening News*, asked readers to send in their stories. Of the countless tales received, the newspaper selected 500 and compiled them into a book that is at once both amusing and poignant. This facsimile edition, complete with the original cartoons provided by famous wartime artist Bert Thomas, is a fitting tribute to the men who risked everything for King and country and whose voices and personalities shine out from the pages of this book.

£9.99 Paperback
70 illustrations
224 pages
978-1-4456-0866-2

Available from all good bookshops or to order direct
Please call **01453-847-800**
www.amberleybooks.com

Also available from Amberley Publishing

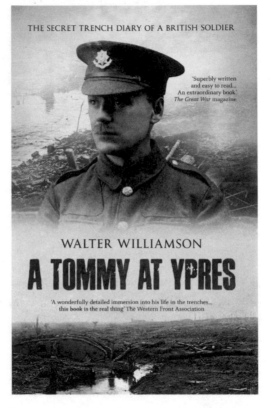

The secret trench diary of a British soldier

'A wonderfully detailed immersion into his life in the trenches ... this book is the real thing. A lovely man; a great read' THE WESTERN FRONT ASSOCIATION

'There was a blinding flash and an ear-splitting report and the "prisoner" fell across me. The bullet had caught him full in the chin and passed out at the base of his skull.'
Within these pages lies the reality of life for a Tommy: the bravery, the warm comradeship, the gentle humour, the strength of character and resilience, the sadness, the tragedy – *A Tommy at Ypres* reveals the true spirit of an outstanding generation.

£12.99 Paperback
25 illustrations
352 pages
978-1-4456-1368-0

Available from all good bookshops or to order direct
Please call **01453-847-800**
www.amberleybooks.com